Disco

GIBRALTAR

Terry Palmer

Heritage House

First published March 1987

ISBN 1852150025

This is one of a series of guide books already published or in preparation.
Titles in the series include:

Discover Gibraltar
Discover The Isle of Man
Discover The Channel Islands
Discover Malta
Discover The Suffolk Coast
Descubre Gibraltar y su Campo (Spanish edition)
Royal Norfolk
Coming down the Stour
Cambridge, Ely & Newmarket
How to Survive on the Costa

Typesetting by Essex Phototypesetting, Clacton
Printed by Paddell Printing Co Ltd
6, Grainger Road, Southend-on-Sea, Essex
Published by Heritage House (Publishers) Ltd
5, King's Road, Clacton-on-Sea

Contents

Terry Palmer's first visit to Gibraltar was in 1963 after spending six months towing a caravan from England. He stayed a month and became fascinated by the Rock and its history. He has been back several times and claims the fascination grows with each visit.

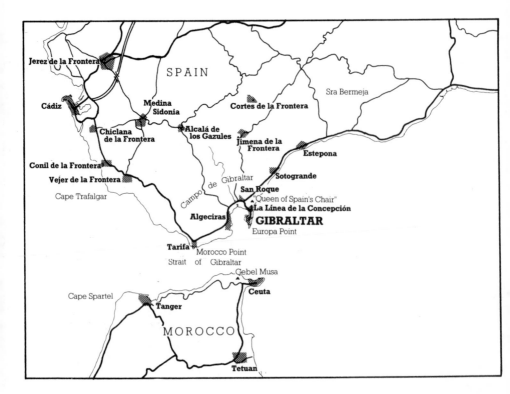

Rock Bottom

AT LATITUDE 36 degrees 7 minutes 16 seconds North, Gibraltar vies with Algeciras for being the second most southerly town in Europe. The most southerly, at 36 degrees exact, is the little settlement of Tarifa, nestling on Punta Marroqui – Morocco Point – with a spectacular view across the strait to north Africa only eight miles (11km) away, and with a history that's tied up with Gibraltar's own.

The Rock, along with Spain, is permanently one hour ahead of British time, BST or GMT, though it lies on longitude 5 degrees 21 minutes 13 seconds West (figures are for the Dockyard clock tower), three minutes east of Hayle in Cornwall.

Money The Rock's official currency is the Gibraltar Pound, at parity with the Pound Sterling. The Government of Gibraltar issues its own currency notes – including the £1 note – with British coinage – including the £1 coin – the legal tender, but as visitors outnumber the native population fifty-fold during the year, many currencies are freely accepted, with the peseta and the US dollar topping the list.

Banks Barclay's Bank has branches in Main Street and Irish Town, Hambro's Bank is by Southport, the Gibraltar-based Galliano's Bank is in Main Street, and banks from several other countries, not including Spain, are represented.

Post and Telephones The Post Office, also in Main Street, is run on British lines, with its own philatelic counter. There are sub-offices in North and South district. Business hours are 9am-1pm, 2pm-5pm (3pm-5pm at sub-offices). STD phone calls can be made from hotels to Britain and most other countries, but not to Spain. Most hotels have call boxes on the public line, but calls going through hotel switchboards cost more than the standard rate. The telephone exchange is between John Mackintosh Square and Line Wall Road

Police The police wear the same uniform as in Britain, and many constables go to Britain for part of their training. Most of the police-force is Gibraltar-born including, for the first time, the Chief Commissioner. The Police Office is in Irish Town.

How big? Gibraltar is small, measuring 5,566 yards (3.16 miles or 5,089 metres) from the middle point of the frontier fence to the southernmost tip, just west of Europa Point lighthouse. Its maximum width, not counting the man-made harbour, is about 1,500 yards (0.85 of a mile or 1,400 metres) from Line Wall Road to the observation platform overlooking Catalan Bay. Yet there are 27 miles (43 km) of road (plus 4.25 miles (6.8 km) of footpath) for thousands of vehicles, which means that parking in the Town is extremely difficult – local people who find a good parking spot are often reluctant to drive away and lose it.

Motoring Observe the yellow-line parking code strictly, and note that double yellow lines sandwiching a pale blue one indicate tow-away zones.

The rule of the road is drive on the *right*, as in all of Continental Europe, which means the Gibraltar Police are among the few British bobbies in the world to have this experience. Petrol is around the same price as in Britain and is available at several stations notably around Winston Churchill Avenue and the approaches to Waterport. There's another on Rosia Road near the dry docks.

Car hire Car hire firms operate in the same area and will allow cars hired on the Rock to be taken to Spain, but a 20-minute walk from Casemates Square, even allowing time to cross the frontier, takes one into the business centre of La Línea de la Concepción where there are other car hire firms, though these vehicles may *not* be taken into Gibraltar. Officially, Spanish car hire firms must ask for an International Driving Licence though in practise this seldom happens.

Since Spain entered the EEC in 1986, car hire has been subjected to VAT at 33%, which makes it uncompetitive with Gibraltar rates. Gib has signed some clauses in the Treaty of Rome but has not accepted total integration into the Common Market and Value Added Tax is *not* added.

Driving laws The Rock's speed limit is 30mph (48kph) maximum, and less in certain areas; wearing of seat belts is *not* compulsory in Gibraltar though it is in Spain, and driving under the influence of alcohol is established on medical evidence in court; there are no blood tests and there's no "breathalyser."

Duty free The duty-free status has long gone, but Gibraltar's shops can still offer spirits at half the British price and the Airport duty-free shop is even cheaper. There is, of course, no VAT, and many shops can arrange tax-free shopping for export.

Gibraltar does not observe the Spanish siesta, and shops normally close around 5pm to 5.30pm, but those catering for the tourist trade stay open late on evenings when a cruise liner is in port.

The Rock enjoys special tax concessions and, like the Channel Islands, the Isle of Man, Andorra, and several islands in the West Indies, is an offshore tax haven for certain international companies.

Basic shopping When the frontier was closed, Gibraltar imported its fruit and vegetables from Portugal and Morocco (and drinking water from Morocco as well). With the frontier open Spanish produce is on sale, but the merchants still deal with their former suppliers. Processed foods from Britain are slightly dearer, having to bear the cost of transport.

Water Gates

Population The population in 1983 was estimated at 29,073, with the great majority of them crowded into the Town, either in old-style stone houses lining steep and narrow streets, or in modern flats, many of them Government-owned – the local equivalent of the British council flat.

Around 20,000 Gibraltarians hold British passports with full right of residence in the United Kingdom. While many people are of Spanish blood, the Gibraltarian family tree includes branches from Genoa, Portugal, Menorca, Malta and Britain, plus Jews who have sought refuge over the years, and with flavourings from throughout the Mediterranean.

Residence People born in EEC countries may stay in Gib for six months if they're looking for work or starting a business; after that they can stay for up to five years on a residence permit which can be renewed. Non-EEC nationals looking for work permits have to satisfy more stringent conditions, particularly on housing and repatriation. Full details are available from the Immigration Officer at 180 Irish Town or the Department of Labour at John Mackintosh Square.

Health UK passport holders are entitled to free treatment in the public wards of St Bernard's Hospital, and less urgent treatment at the health centre on Casemates Square; medical treatment elsewhere, plus all dental care (except for extractions in normal business hours at St Bernard's) must be paid for. Citizens of other EEC states, including Ireland, need a form E111 available in their home country.

Housing Incomers have to compete with residents for housing, which is expensive because of the pressure on space. Nonetheless, Gib has a dozen estate agents, many of whom also deal with property in Spain.

Language English is the official language but Spanish is very widely spoken. The average Gibraltarian is more at home in Spanish; the more recent weekly newspapers use both languages, but the old-established *Gibraltar Chronicle* sticks mainly to English. Spanish television is available as an alternative to the English-language programmes of the Gibraltar Broadcasting Corporation, screened from 7pm nightly on Channel Six. GBC's radio programmes come in both languages.

Air travel GB Airways in association with British Airways oprates one or two daily services between the Rock and Gatwick, though the aircraft sometimes has the Britannia Airways livery. Gibair also flies its own Viscount "Yogibair" (Yogi Bear – get it?) on a twice-daily (excluding Sunday) 20-minute service to Tanger and on special charters to south European cities. Air Europe runs daily scheduled services from Gatwick and Manchester. There are plans to increase the routes into the Rock.

The visitor coming to Gib by air will find a smart but tiny terminal with two check-in desks, restaurant, duty-free shop – and a bus and taxi rank outside. But it's only a ten-minute walk to Main Street, even with hand luggage.

There are no airport taxes to pay.

When a Hercules transport lands the whole town hears it

If you decide to walk into Town don't drop any litter, because Winston Churchill Avenue (this part of it used to be called Road to Spain until General Franco closed the border) crosses the runway, a feature unique in the world (unless you know another). The airfield is unusual for other reasons; at its eastern end, by the Mediterranean, it goes to within a few feet of the frontier fence, while its western end extends well out into the Bay, built on limestone excavated from within the Rock during the Second World War. The runway is 2,000 yards (1,830 metres) long, not enough to take the biggest passenger jets.

Civil aircraft share the runway with the military but the RAF has its own terminal buildings. In the early 1980s a Vulcan bomber, "City of Gibraltar," went on permanent display where the road crosses the runway, and in May 1986, after the British and American bombing raid on Libya, aircraft-carrier-style arrester wires were fitted to the runway to allow Phantom jets to land.

Planes approaching or taking off over the Bay must not overfly Spanish territory, hence they bank steeply for a run in or out on a north-south line, giving passengers an excellent view of the Rock – or the sky over Algeciras.

The Bay Depending on where you live, the Bay is called either Bahía de Algeciras or Bay of Gibraltar. Throughout this book it is known as the Bay. Spanish pronunciation, by the way, calls for *G* to be pronounced like the *CH* in the Scottish word *loch*, hence to English-attuned ears it is *AlHethiras* and **H**ibraltar, with the stress on the *tar*.

Sea travel Bland Line, owner of Gibair, runs the 45-minute hydrofoil service from Waterport Wharf to Algeciras and on to Tanger, and the *Mons Calpe* car ferry, crossing direct to Tanger in 2.5hrs. The car ferry will bring you back the same day, but the hydrofoil will not.

The launch *Coronia*, a veteran of the Dunkirk evacuation, runs dolphin safaris in the Bay and cruises around the Rock, offering wonderful views of Gibraltar from the sea.

You can also reach north Africa from Spain, either by catching the Bland hydrofoil at Algeciras for Tanger, or taking another Algeciras service to Ceuta, a Spanish enclave on the Moroccan coast visible from Catalan Bay and Europa Point on clear days. And from Tarifa a hydrofoil goes across to Tanger.

The Frontier The land crossing, closed on May 2, 1968, and reopened for unrestricted travel in 1985, is by far the easiest, though there can be the problem of queues at peak times. Three dual carriageways cross what was once the Spanish half of the neutral territory, converging at the Gibraltar gates from where Winston Churchill Avenue takes over.

In the first year of the reopened frontier almost a million people came in through the gates, most of them on foot and most with minimum formality.

Weather Gibraltar has around 35 inches (900mm) of rain a year, almost twice that of London, but most of it falls from October to March and even then it comes in heavy storms rather than in all-day drizzle. Summer rainfall is exclusively in thunderstorms, and I recall seeing an impressive display of St Elmo's Fire at La Línea during a thunderstorm in March 1963. Snow is extremely rare on the Rock but occasionally whitens the mountains of The Rif in Morocco.

The maximum temperature in January averages 64°F (18°C) but the rare bleak wind blowing off the cold Spanish mountains can send the mercury down to freezing point. The average maximum for July comes out at a comfortable 85°F (29°C).

With the easterly wind, the Levanter, the rain catchments come into their own, and the steep eastern side of the Rock creates its own cloud which can plunge the Town into shade all day, while elsewhere the skies are blue.

Where to stay Hotels, arranged in approximate descending price order are: **Rock** (Europa Road, tel 73000), **Holiday Inn** (Governor's Parade, 70500), **Caleta Palace** (Catalan Bay, 76501), **Continental** (Engineer Lane, 76900), **Bristol** (Cathedral Square, 76800), **Montarik** (Main Street, 77065), **Queen's** (Boyd Street,74000).

Self-catering apartments are at **Ocean Heights** (Montagu Place, 75548) and **Both Worlds Aparthotel** (Sandy Bay, 76191).

Bed and breakfast in private homes is not available due to pressure on housing. There are no camping sites on Gib, though there are several within a few miles in Spain. Caravans are not allowed into Gibraltar unless in transit, using the *Mons Calpe* car ferry.

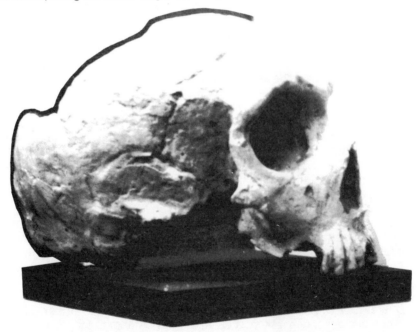

The Gibraltar skull – but this is a replica

Rock of Ages

AN EARLY Gibraltar resident died on the scree which tumbled down the steep slope beneath where the so-called Moorish Castle now stands. In 1843 his, or her, skull was found and taken to London with few people giving second thoughts to the discovery. Thirteen years later when a similar skull was found in the Neander Valley in Germany, archaeologists named him Neanderthal Man, and the history of the human race jumped back to 40,000 years BC.

By then the skull of a child had also been found on Gibraltar and casts of this and the first skull, both now recognised as belonging to Neanderthal Man, are in the Gibraltar Museum.

Neanderthal, followed by Cro-Magnon man, occupied several of the hundred natural caves on the Rock, and life-sized models of Neander and Neolithic humans, made by Berman and Nathan of London, now occupy deep recesses of St Michael's Cave on the Upper Rock.

St Michael's Cave The cave, with an entrance 900 feet (300 metres) above sea level, is one of the modern tourist attractions. Its grand hall has a concrete floor and seating for several hundred people who can enjoy concerts with the music resonating around the stalactites. During the Hitler War troops converted the grand hall into an emergency hospital, hence the modern floor, but St Michael's never received any patients. The blastings revealed another cave, New St Michael's, which plunges deep into the limestone and ends in a lake, but to explore this for any distance you must be a skilled potholer as there are considerable dangers. In fact, neither the blastings nor the explorers have found the bodies of two Army officers who went potholing in St Michael's in 1840 and were never seen again.

Pillars of Hercules Pottery and glass relics found in the recesses show that the Phoenecians knew St Michael's Cave around 800BC, though they never settled on the Rock, seeing it and its twin, Gebel Musa in Morocco – Mount Abyla and Ape's Hill are its other names – as the Pillars of Hercules, marking the end of the known world.

The Phoenecians believed that Atlas, who supported the world on his back, was not far beneath this spot, hence the naming of the Atlas Mountains in Morocco. And the name Iberia, for the land-mass of Spain,

11

Portugal, Andorra and Gibraltar, derives from the Phoenecian word *eber* meaning "ultimate," "furthest." Cautious, the Phoenecians preferred to build their settlement of Carteia at the mouth of the tiny River Guadarranque at the head of the Bay, naming it from their god Melcart.

Roman conquest The Romans knew of the Rock as Mons Calpe, believing it to be hollow. They also called it *non plus ultra* meaning "there is no beyond," but when the Spaniards discovered in 1492 that there was quite a lot "beyond" they took for their national motto *plus ultra*. After all, they owned most of it.

The Romans, too, declined to occupy the Rock, probably because it was waterless. They settled in Carteia which became a base for fishermen and for distillers of purple dye, extracted from shellfish and used to colour the imperial toga. Carteia was the birthplace of Pomponius Mela, the Roman mapmaker.

The Roman rule ended when the Goths and the Vandals invaded Iberia from the north between 409 and 415, and what had been the Hispanic province of Baetica became the Kingdom of Andalucia, perpetuating the Vandal name for eternity.

The Gothic King Recared, who ruled from 586 to 601, converted Iberia to Christianity and built a church on the knifeback ridge of the Rock at Middle Hill, and another a few miles inland where centuries later the Spaniards were to found the town of San Roque under unhappy circumstances. Recared, or his successors, established the provincial capital of Asido, inland from the Roman port of Gades, later to be called Cádiz.

But the limestone rock at the southern tip of Europe still had no strategic value, though the Visigothic King Witiza laid the course for change when he put Roderic, the Count of Córdoba, in command of his army, for in 710 Roderic rebelled and deposed Witiza, whose sons fled across the strait to Ceuta.

Count Julian, the Vizigothic Governor of Ceuta, who had managed to hold off the advancing supporters of Islam, saw this as his chance of revenge, for his wife Faldrina was Witiza's daughter, and his own daughter Florina had been seduced by Roderic while she was maid of honour at his court. Julian thus sought the help of the Emir Musa ibn Nosseyr, the Moorish Governor of North Africa deputising for the all-powerful Caliph of Damascus, and suggested Europe was ripe for Islamic conquest.

Looking at the situation 12 centuries later one must assume Count Julian was either incompetent or mad, for how could he hope to hold onto Christian Ceuta when all around him were land-grabbing Moslems?

Tarifa By September, Musa had gathered 500 men, whom he sent from Tanger to Europe under the command of Tarif abu Zara. They landed at the southernmost tip of the continent where the Romans had founded the 'town of Traducta – it's now called Tarifa from its conqueror – and ravaged the countryside. In later centuries this souvenir of Tarif's visit was to have a castle to guard the sea lanes to the Mediterranean, sometimes charging a *tariff* for the right of passage.

But in 710 Tarif reported that Europe was wide open to invasion, and in April of 711 Musa sent the Persian warrior Tarik ibn Zeyad from Bellynch, near Ceuta, across to Andalucia with 500 cavalry and between 7,000 and 12,000 Berber foot soldiers. Tarik struck first at Algeciras then became the first person in history to recognise that the rocky peninsula opposite formed a natural fortress. He therefore sailed across the Bay, landed near what is today's Rosia Road at the base of the Alameda Gardens, and occupied the promontory.

Guzman El Bueno's castle at Tarifa

He quickly found that Tarif's judgement was an understatement: Iberia was deplorably badly defended. Tarik marched inland a few miles, defeated the Visigothic King Roderic near Asido, helped by the defection of half Roderic's forces, then he swept northward capturing almost everything in his path. Some cities fell only after a prolonged siege but the only real resistance came from the people in a remote part of the Cantabrian Mountains on the Biscay coast. Tarik, with his polyglot army of Arabs, Berbers, Moors and Syrians, bypassed them, crossed the Pyrenees, and took the Moslem invasion half way up France until he was checked at the Battle of Poitiers in 732.

The Visigothic town of Asido was to become the Moorish Medina Sidonia, and it's pure chance that the old name is sandwiched in the new. Medina Sidonia was the city, *mdina*, for the new immigrants from Sidon,

Cannon at Alameda

now in The Lebanon. The name Palestine, blended to *Filistin*, was applied to this southern part of Iberia, giving us the word *philistine* to go with our *vandal* and *barbartic*.

Meanwhile, the victorious Moors had paid their debt to Count Julian of Ceuta for his brillant idea. They stoned his wife to death, threw his son from the castle ramparts, and left the count to die in irons in a prison deep in the Pyrenean foothills.

And Tarik ordered the first miltary defences on what was now his mountain. The Moorish Castle has been rebuilt several times over the ages and bears no relation to what Tarik created. But Tarik's Mountain is still *Gebel Tarik*, though today we spell it *Gibraltar*.

Tarik's Rock

THE ISLAMIC invaders were on the Rock for 727 years and in Iberia for 781, most of the time fighting a rearguard action as the Christians emerged from their hideouts in the Cantabrian Mountains and began the reconquest of their land. Over the centuries they formed little kingdoms, as in León, Asturias, Aragon and Navarra, but gradually they consolidated themselves into the Portuguese on the Atlantic, the Catalans on the Mediterranean, and in the middle the Castillians, named from the vast castles they built to hold their newly-won territory against reprisal attacks from the Moslem south, and occasionally from their Christian allies.

The three Iberian races evolved their own languages from the dog Latin of the Roman era, but as they gradually absorbed the conquered lands of Islam their languages and culture took on an Arab influence, particularly noticeable in Castilla, which ultimately became Spain, and most noticeable in modern Spanish words beginning with *al*, Arabic for "the" – as in *álgebra* and *álcali* (alkali), which have spread into English.

During their long dominion in what they called *al-Ándalus*, the invaders from Barbary proved they were not completely barbaric by creating some of the most beautiful architecture in the country, notably the Court of the Lions in Granada, the mosque in Córdoba, and the Giralda (weathervane) tower in Sevilla.

But on Gibraltar the architecture was much more functional. Tarik's immediate successors strengthened his castle overlooking the isthmus, and by 1160 the fortress was large, but the ruins you see today, extending down the mountainside almost to the edge of Casemates Square, are from later periods in the Islamic occupation.

Caliph of Damascus Gibraltar, meanwhile, was becoming involved in the internal squabbles of the ruling Moors, as in 741 when Abd al Malic gained control of al-Andalus for the Caliph of Damascus. He was so unpopular that the Faithful invited Abd al Kajez to come from north Africa and overthrow him. Malic defeated the upstart Kajez on the banks of the Guadiana River and Kajez retreated to Córdoba, to Gibraltar, and finally back to Africa.

Northern Europe was still lost in the Dark Ages, but the Emperor Charlemagne crossed the Pyrenees in 778 for his first attack on al-

15

The Rock from Europa Point

Andalus. His son recaptured Barcelona in 801 and by 950 the Christians had regained territory from Pôrto (Oporto) to Pamplona.

Al-Andalus collapsed in 1031 as a sovereign state, giving way to divided rule; the Berber emirates held lands from mid-Portugal to Almería, including Gibraltar; the Arab Emirates were on the Mediterranean coast, and the Umayyad Caliphate was squeezed in the middle.

The Emir of Sevilla emerged as quasi-independent ruler of the Umayyad, though forced to pay tribute to the Christians north of him. In desperation, and against advice, he begged the help of the Caliph of Morocco, Yusef ibn Taxfin, leader of the Almorávides, the people "vowed to God."

Yusef seized Gibraltar, Algeciras, and then all of Moslem Spain, and sent the disillusioned emir into exile in a Saharan oasis while he persecuted all but the hardline Muslims. Jews by the thousand fled north into Christian Iberia, taking a number of Christians with them.

Eventually the Almohades, the "unitarians" practising religious tolerance, crossed from Africa to Gibraltar to replace Yusef's doctrine. Their leader, Abd al Mumin ibn Ali, began building the city of Medina al Fath, the "City of Victory" on the Rock, which he renamed Gebel al Fath, the "Mountain of Victory."

Moorish baths The name of Tarik, the victor, still proved more popular than the victory itself, and the name Gebel al Fath was lost, as was most of the City of Victory. Apart from the castle, the only inanimate Moorish remains on the Rock today are a watchtower high on the watershed; the ·Chapel of Our Lady of Europa, which began life as a mosque; the hint of a jetty near the yacht marina; and the Moorish baths, preserved in the floor of the Gibraltar Museum.

16

Barbary Apes There are some well-known animate remains, because at some stage in their dominion, the Moors brought over specimens of *macaca sylvana*, the Barbary ape, which is really a monkey without a tail. Legend claims that these monkeys found their own way to the Rock through a natural tunnel under the strait, but this is as fanciful as pigs that fly.

Legend also claims that as long as the "apes" inhabit the Rock, it will remain under British rule. The macaques themselves raise a serious scientific poser when we ask why they are confined to Tarik's Mountain when they could have followed Tarik's example and colonised all of al-Andalus.

El Cid While the followers of Mahomet squabbled in the south, the Christians, though doing their own squabbling in the north, managed to capture more territory. In 1094 Ruy Díaz de Bivar, better known as El Cid (from the Arabic *sidi*, "lord"), seized Valencia for himself, and the Kingdom of León and Castilla reached Toledo. Between 1236 and 1248 the Christians captured Córdoba and Sevilla, and the Muwahid Caliphate in al-Andalus was reduced to the strip from Cádiz to Alicante, based on Granada and including Spain's most majestic mountains, the Sierra Nevada.

The modern map of Spain shows evidence of this part of the reconquest in the towns which still keep their frontier image: Jerez de la Frontera and, coming ever closer to the Rock, Chiclana, Conil, and Vejer all claiming to be "de la Frontera."

First Siege In 1309 Ferdinand of Castilla (not *the* Ferdinand who married Isabella) decided to push the frontier deeper into the lands of the caliphate. He sent Alonzo Perez de Guzman – Guzman "el Bueno" – to attack Gibraltar. After a short siege the Rock fell to the Christians and for the first time in its history, Gibraltar was under Spanish rule.

Guzman the Good retired to Tarifa and built a large castle overlooking the strait and the tiny island which lies at the southernmost tip of Europe. In modern times the island has been connected to the remainder of the continent by a causeway, but Guzman's castle still stands proud, overlooking what is now Tarifa's hydrofoil basin.

Gibraltar, however, was not to remain Spanish for long. Ferdinand had offered asylum on the Rock to thieves, murderers, and women who had escaped from their husbands, but Tarik's Mountain was by now of great significance to the shrinking Emirate of Granada, all that remained of the Islamic empire in Europe.

Second and Third Sieges Ismail ibn Ferag laid the second siege in 1315, but had to withdraw. Mohammed IV brought troops over from north Africa for the third siege in 1333, and after 18 weeks Don Vasco Perez de Meiras, who had used his defence allocation to buy vineyards at Jerez, surrendered the Rock to Islam. But Mohammed didn't enjoy his victory for long; he was assassinated and Abul Hassan, the Sultan of Fez, seized control. Six hundred and fifty years later his namesake, Sir Joshua Hassan, was the elected leader of the Gibraltar Government. There is a subtle difference, however: Sir Joshua is a Jew.

Tower of Homage The Moors and Berbers, reinhabiting the Rock in 1333, rebuilt the ruined castle and added the Tower of Homage at the highest point. In the years that followed, the fortress has all but vanished and what is popularly called the Moorish Castle is in reality just this Tower of Homage. Its upper floors are open to visitors, with access from Willis's Road, but few people are invited into the tower's basement: it's now the Gibaltar Prison.

Fourth Siege King Ferdinand's successor Alfonso XI vowed to win back Gibraltar for the Crown. While Abul Hassan was at work on the tower Alfonso managed to land troops near Europa Point but despite besieging the Town and castle for ten weeks, the fourth siege failed.

In 1342 Alfonso laid siege to Algeciras with an army that included several English knights searching for fresh adventures now the Crusades were over. The siege featured the first recorded use of gunpowder in Europe, and Algeciras quickly fell to the Spaniards.

Fifth Siege Alfonso tried again to take Gibraltar, but the seven-month fifth siege of 1349 was another failure. The following year Alfonso died of plague and while his successor, Peter I, more descriptively known as Pedro the Cruel, began slaughtering his fellow Spaniards, including his wife, the defenders of Gibraltar could rest awhile.

There was a relatively small incident in which Pedro murdered a friendly king of Granada for the sake of his large ruby. Pedro gave the stone to the English Black Prince who had come to fight with him, and the stone eventually became the main jewel in the English Crown. The Granadans, mourning their king, sailed from Gibraltar and sacked Algeciras.

Sixth Siege In 1411 the people of Gibraltar turned against their Granadan rulers, drove them out of the Town, and handed themselves and the Rock to the king of Morocco who garrisoned the fortress with 1,000 horse and 2,000 men. But Yussuf of Granada didn't like the idea and after a short sixth siege, recaptured the peninsula.

Seventh Siege The Spaniards laid the seventh siege in August 1436 but its commander, Enrique de Guzman, the Count of Niebla, drowned while trying to save his landing party. He had come ashore near the present Alameda Gardens and didn't know the Moors had built a wall at the south end of the Town. The defenders put his body in a casket and hung it from the battlements of the castle where it was to remain for many years.

Eighth Siege And then came the eighth siege. Alonzo de Arcos, the Alcalde (Mayor) of Tarifa, with another Enrique de Guzman, Duke of Medina Sidonia and son of the man hanging in the casket, led the attack and on August 20, 1462, the Rock was again in Spanish hands, where it would stay for the next 242 years.

Just 30 years later, as Christopher Columbus was discovering the "plus ultra" of the New World, Ferdinand of Aragon and Isabella of Castilla, now king and queen of a unified Spain, captured Granada and ended the 781 years of Islamic occupation of Iberia.

Spanish Rock

THE SPANIARDS took the surrender of Gibraltar on August 20, 1462, St Bernard's Day – Bernard has been the Rock's patron saint ever since – and at once Enrique de Guzman began garrisoning the town and castle according to the custom of the age. King Henry (Enrique) IV of Castilla decided Guzman was being too presumptuous and reserved his rewards for Alonzo; Arcos's tomb in the Carthusian Monastery in Sevilla refers to him as "much honoured" and recalls that he recovered Gibraltar "from the enemies of the faith" without mentioning friend Guzman.

Henry declared the territory for 29 leagues around the Rock to be the Campo de Gibraltar, the first time this expression appears. Then he annexed Gibraltar town and its campo for himself.

Henry visited the Rock in 1463 and raised his friend Beltran de la Cueva to Alcalde, and Estevan de Villacreces as military governor of the new territory.

Ninth Siege Anarchy hit Spain in 1465 and the 11-year-old Infante Don Alonzo, nominated king by his supporters, gave the title of Gibraltar and the Campo back to the Duke of Medina Sidonia, who immediately laid the ninth siege to regain possession.

The defender, Estevan de Villacreces, was driven slowly from the fringes of the town, moving to the castle, but as Medina Sidonia's troops gradually advanced he took final refuge in the Tower of Homage where he held out for the last five months of the 15-month siege. King Henry acknowledged the status and signed a royal decee in 1469 agreeing to the duke's hold on El Peñon (the name the Spanish familiarly give to the Rock: it means "cliff" or "peak") but reserved for himself the sovereign seigniorial rights. Among Medina Sidonia's first actions when he entered the Town was to remove the body of his father which had been hanging in that casket for 29 years.

Gibraltar Coat of Arms During the siege of Granada in 1492 when Ferdinand and Isabella were at the Christian stronghold of Santa Fé (Holy Faith) waiting for the defeat of the Moors, the Gibraltarians asked the Crown for a coat of arms. Legend claims that Isabella, passing the time at Santa Fé, personally embroidered a banner, using gold thread on red damask about a yard square. She created a heraldic emblem featuring a three-turreted castle with a large key hanging beneath it, symbolising Gibraltar's role as the Key of the Spanish dominions. A crown sits above the emblem, and a symbolic wreath enfolds it, creating a work of art which is impressive in its beauty half a millennium later.

Isabella was not so obliging when on the death of Enrique, Duke of Medina Sidonia, in that same year of 1492, his son Juán de Guzman asked for confirmation of his title to El Peñon and the Campo.

The joint monarchs, ecstatic at having driven the last of the Infidel from their land, were in no mood to weaken their title to Gibraltar, particularly in view of its new symbolism. They offered the Campo in perpetuity, but only if the duke would renounce his claim to El Peñon itself.

The new Duke of Medina Sidonia refused and stayed in disputed possession of the Rock. In 1497 he even helped Their Catholic Majesties, as the Spanish Pope Alexander VI had now invested Ferdinand and Isabella, take Melilla in north Africa from the Moors, establishing in the process the military and naval importance of the fortress of Gibraltar. Isabella noticed how strategic El Peñon had become and in 1502 she demanded the restoration of the sovereign seigniorial rights and without waiting for a reply annexed Gibraltar to the Crown of Spain.

Tenth Siege Two years later, with Isabella dead, Juán de Guzman blockaded Gibraltar in the tenth siege, but after four months with no progress he relented and at a ceremony in the Ataranza, now Casemates Square, he compensated every Gibraltarian for damages incurred. Ferdinand, acting as regent for Isabella's daughter Juana, added a bonus by describing the citizens of Gibraltar as "most loyal" and reminding them that Isabella's will had specifically stated that El Peñon should never again be separated from the Spanish Crown.

In 1540 Barbarossa's Turkish pirates, led by the corsair Hali Hamat, landed on Dead Man's Beach at the southernmost tip of the Rock and in four hours on an August day plundered and pillaged the Town, taking almost 900 people as slaves, though many others escaped by hiding in the Tower of Homage. The Turks crossed the Bay to repeat the devastation at several points before sailing on to Cartagena where a squadron of Spanish ships attacked them and released 837 of the prisoners. But the message of the day was plain: Gibraltar's southern defences were lacking.

Charles V's Wall Isabella's grandson, the Holy Roman Emperor Charles V, who had become Charles (Carlos) I of Spain on Ferdinand's death, came to Gibraltar and ordered the building of two walls which feature prominent in the defences to this day. The lower part of Charles V's Wall started at the southern end of the already-existing Line Wall at a point beside where Hambro's Bank now stands, and in impressive splendour reached half way up the Rock to meet the base of the crumbling Moorish Wall. A sign in Prince Edward's Road, where it pierces the masonry, recalls that before the new wall was built, the south part of town, La Turba, had its own wall. But it was obviously not good enough.

Another sign nearby quotes the original version of a popular jingle:

God and the soldier all men adore
In time of trouble and no more.
For when war is over and all things righted,
God is neglected and the old soldier slighted.

Southport Southport Gate, the opening in the wall at the end of Main Street, carries Charles's coat of arms over the oldest archway, as well as a modern version of the Gibraltar crest that Isabella created in 1492.

Charles then built the spectacular wall which reaches from the Apes' Den to the watershed almost 1,200 feet above sea level, with three zigzag breaks. The modern visitor climbing the steps worked into this wall has a view that is breathtaking in two senses of the word.

In 1575 Philip (Felipe) II of Spain, who had called himself King of England after his marriage to Mary Tudor 20 years earlier, ordered a small section of wall to complete the southern defences.

Gibraltar was becoming the most fortified town on the Spanish coast, and even had fortifications looking out towards the isthmus and the rest of Spain.

By 1618 the South Mole was beginning to creep out into the Bay to protect shipping from the prevailing south-westerly storms. In 1620 the Torre del Puerto (Port Tower) went up at the base of this mole, and the defence was considered so important the Torre even had its own

Southport Gates

governor and garrison. Finally, complementing the many guns that bristled all over the Rock, the bastions of Santa Cruz and King's were built on the Line Wall, and Rosario Bastion rose near Southport.

Landport Landport was strengthened, leading through the Grand Battery which still dominates the north side of Casemates Square. A footpath now traces the route of this important gateway, but the main entrance to the present-day Town is through the Casemates Gates.

During this activity on El Peñon, Spain was increasing its territories worldwide. Fransisco Pizarro, born to a serving maid in Trujillo, overthrew the Inca and became the conqueror of Peru, and King Felipe had taken Portugal into the Spanish Crown on realising he would never succeed with his claims to the English throne.

Carlos the Bewitched In the next century the reverses were to come. Portugal regained its sovereignty – and in 1662 it ceded Tanger to England as part of the dowry of Catherine of Bragança on her wedding to Charles II. The English abandoned Tanger in 1684; had they not, the history of Gibraltar may well have taken a completely different course. And the Spanish Crown accelerated its decline when Carlos the Bewitched took the reins of monarchy.

In October of 1700 Carlos weakened the already feeble authority of the sovereign when he bequeathed his entire domains, including Flanders, the Indies, the Americas, Sicily and parts of the Italian peninsula to 17-year-old Philip of Anjou, the son of his elder sister, Maria Théresa. If Philip declined, the entire inheritance was to go to the offspring of Carlos's next sister, Margaret. That chain of devolution ended with the Archduke Charles, son of the Elector of Bavaria.

Philip of Anjou was in his native France when he accepted the offer of the Spanish Crown and all that went with it. But he was not master in his own house; he was under the influence of his child-bride Marie-Louise of Savoy, who took her opinions from the Princesse des Ursins, French-born widow of a Spanish grandee. And the princess, in her turn, was answerable to Louis XIV of France.

The idea of merging Spain into the French Crown went against the interests of most other European countries, and the Holy Roman Emperor, now a German, invaded the Italian peninsula to seize the Spanish territories of Naples and Sicily.

War of the Spanish Succession England and the Netherlands signed an alliance with the Emperor in September 1701, committing themselves to defeating the accession of this Philip, who in Spain would be Felipe V, in favour of the other contender, Archduke Charles (Carl) of Austria, who would be Carlos III if he made it.

Prince Georg of Darmstadt had gone to Spain in 1695 with the Imperial Army to resist further French influence and had succeeded to a degree, for Carlos the Bewitched had made him a grandee and his Viceroy in Cataluña. Georg, naturally, disapproved of Felipe as king, and Felipe's first action on setting foot in Spain was, understandably, to dismiss Georg.

In retaliation, Georg went to England to suggest the English attack

The approach to Waterport

Cádiz; then he went on to Portugal to talk that country's King Pedro into supporting this new English-Dutch-German initiative.

The attack on Cádiz failed, but the allied fleet managed to steal silver bullion from the Spanish Main on its way to Vigo; the two incidents became the opening gambits in the War of the Spanish Succession, which was to alter the course of history for the Rock of Gibraltar.

In 1703 Portugal renounced its agreement with France and offered the Alliance a land base for an attack on Spain from the west. The disaffected Catalans, it was thought, would support their erstwhile viceroy and form the other side of a pincer attack.

Two Kings With this groundwork done, Archduke Charles was proclaimed in Vienna as King Carlos III of Spain, which thus had two claimants to the throne.

Carlos went to England and took passage with Sir George Rooke for Lisbon, in advance of his invasion force of 10,000 men and 188 ships. Sir George had led the combined English and Dutch fleets to victory in 1692 in the Battle of la Hogue, off Cherbourg, destroying 15 French ships, but the next year he had suffered a defeat in the Mediterranean at the hands of the French, who had decimated a convoy he was protecting.

Fire Ships As an aside to the main issue, let's look at a little incident which involved Gibraltar. Some of Rooke's merchantmen made it to El Peñon and with Spanish permission took cover behind the new South

Mole. The French, who were supposed to be Spain's allies, sent fire ships into the port to try to drive out the English, but the mole proved the perfect defence against this old strategy.

Sir George landed his royal passenger in Portugal and sailed on to Barcelona with Prince Georg and 1,800 of his troops, to lead the insurrection in the east. Portugal's military proved so unfit for combat that the western prong of the attack never materialised – and in the east, Prince Georg, the former viceroy, could not induce the Catalans to support his new king, this Carlos III.

Rooke therefore sailed away in disillusion and by mid July was aboard the flagship *Royal Catherine* off Tetuan, Morocco, wondering what to do next to revive not only the fortunes of the ailing Carlos cause, but also the job prospects of Sir George himself.

Suddenly the idea came to him: he would capture Gibraltar.

Queen Isabella's royal coat of arms at Southport Gates

24

Rooke's Rock

ON JULY 21 – August 1 according to the Spanish, who had adopted the Gregorian calendar – Sir George Rooke sailed 50 warships and 70 transports ships into the Bay and dropped anchor. In the afternoon Prince Georg of Darmstadt landed on the isthmus with 1,800 marines, cut off land communication with the remainder of Spain, and called on the Governor of Gibraltar, Diego Salinas, to surrender in the name of Carlos III. Thus began the eleventh siege.

Salinas replied that the town and the garrison were loyal to Felipe V and that he would therefore fight. He controlled a fortress of formidable proportions with the Lengua del Diablo (Devil's Tongue) Battery at the base of the Old Mole, Tuerto (One-eyed), at the New Mole, San Joaquin below the Moorish Castle, and the Luna Creciente (Half Moon) near the foot of King Charles V's Wall. He had enough food, but water, as always, was a problem, and according to a concensus of the varying English figures he had only around 150 men, less than half of them fully trained, and including six cavalrymen without horses. He also had around 120 guns, some of which were almost obsolete. He was also dangerously low on powder and shot. English figures also claim he had 6,000 civilians, a liability and a drain on the rations, but Spanish figures, as we shall see, tell a slightly different story.

Eleventh Siege Rooke planned to attack on July 22 (Aug 2) but the Levanter wind kept his fleet in the Bay with no chance of making a landing. Thus the first real day of this, the eleventh siege, was on July 23 (Aug 3), when Prince Georg's troops sent warning shots over the town in the early morning, followed by a barrage of 15,000 cannonballs in the next six hours.

Jumper's Bastion Captain Hicks landed on the New Mole (the southern one) and was advancing past a magazine called Leandro when it blew up, killing or maiming around 100 of his men and destroying the Tuerto Battery. Soon after, Captain Whittaker with 200 or 300 marines landed near Rosia Bay and advanced into the town along the Line Wall to seize the Santa Cruz Bastion, which he renamed Jumper's Bastion after one of the men killed in Hicks's landing party.

Prince Georg was pushing home his attack from the isthmus and again called on Governor Diego Salinas to surrender, but again Salinas refused. The fighting subsided at nightfall and on the morning of the fourth day, July 24 (Aug 4), Salinas acknowledged resistance was useless and he negotiated an honourable surrender, allowing his garrison to march out with its baggage, three cannon and 36 cannonballs. The townspeople were given the choice of staying and swearing allegiance to the new King Carlos III, or going.

Nuestra Señora de Europa In effect there was little choice, particularly after the civil population had seen their womenfolk mauled by the English, and learned that the statue of the Virgin Mary in the shrine of Our Lady of Europa, had been hurled into the sea. There was also the question of what would happen if supporters of King Felipe should recapture El Peñon and learn that its people had renounced him as their sovereign.

But the vital point must be made: Rooke had not seized Gibraltar for *England*. He had taken it in the name of King Carlos, and the Rock was still *Spanish*. There is disagreement on whether he changed his mind, for some reports state that at the surrender Carlos's flag went up in place of the Spanish standard, soon to be hauled down in favour of the cross of St George of England.

Sir Clowdisley Shovell A fortnight later Rooke sailed with his 50 ships, met the French fleet off Málaga and fought another indecisive battle, hampered by lack of ammunition: too much of it had gone into bombarding El Peñon. Rooke came back to the Rock to refit, then sailed off to England and a lukewarm reception. Meanwhile, Sir Clowdisley Shovell with a squadron of English and German troops captured Barcelona and went on to take Valencia and Aragon and – eventually – Madrid, before being driven back to the sea.

Twelfth Siege Down at the southern tip of Spain, the troops of Felipe V quickly tried to recapture Gibraltar from the supporters of Carlos III. By October of 1704 around 7,000 Spanish and French soldiers – some reports put the total at 12,000 – had gathered on the isthmus and dug themselves in, while 12 French ships of the line and seven frigates lay in the Bay. On October 15 (Oct 26) on the orders of their commander the Marquis de Villadarías, the troops opened fire with cannon.

Shepherd's Path One of the most ingenious and daring attacks of all the sieges of Gibraltar happened in the early hours of October 31 (Nov 10) when 500 volunteers under Colonel Figueroa climbed the precipitous eastern face of the Rock in darkness via the *Senda del Pastor*, the Shepherd's Path, which a traitorous goatherd by name of Simon Susarte had pointed out. The party spent the remainder of the night in St Michael's Cave, stormed over Charles V's Wall at daybreak and slaughtered the guard at Middle Hill, near where the cable car upper terminus now stands.

There was fierce fighting as they tried to enter the town, and Prince Henry of Hesse, brother of Prince Georg of Darmstadt, was injured, but the attackers were forced to surrender when they ran out of ammunition, their expected follow-up of 1,500 men failed to make it up the *senda*, the

Waterport

diversionary attack from the north was called off, and a squadron from the British Navy prevented the planned attack from the sea.

The siege dragged on into the winter, when heavy rains made conditions on the isthmus near impossible for the attackers, hindered too by several sorties by the defenders. In despair Felipe V withdrew Villadarías and replaced him with a French commander, Maréchal Tessé, who brought in a squadron of 18 French ships in February to blockade the Rock.

But it was already too late, for the garrison was up to the comfortable strength of 4,000 men and there was no way the siege could have succeeded without contining the blockade for months. On April 18 (Apr 29) Tessé acknowledged defeat and retired from the isthmus.

The twelfth siege had cost the attackers 70,000 shot, 8,000 cannonballs, and 10,000 men, most of them to disease: the garrison lost 400 men. And when it was all over they erased every trace of the Shepherd's Path.

The War of the Spanish Succession dragged on for several years until Archduke Charles's brother died and Charles suddenly became Emperor of Austria, Italy and Belgium. There was a sudden reversal in English thinking as politicians decided this was not now the man they wanted to see take control of the Spanish dominions as well as what he now held, and England pulled out of the Alliance.

There was one little problem. English troops were holding Gibraltar for the king England no longer supported. The question of the Rock's future was eventually settled by negotiation at the Treaty of Utrecht in 1713.

Under this treaty, which is on display in the Palace of Versailles, Austria took the Spanish Netherlands and parts of Italy, which went well with Charles's new territory, and Felipe V kept everything else except Gibraltar and Menorca, both of which he ceded to the occupying power, England – or rather Britain, as the Act of Union was now in effect.

Treaty of Utrecht Article X of the treaty says in the official English translation of the Latin original:

The Catholic King does hereby, for Himself, His heirs and successors, yield to the Crown of Great Britain the full and intire propriety of the Town and Castle of Gibraltar, together with the port, fortifications and forts thereunto belonging; and He gives up the said propriety, to be held and enjoyed absolutely with all manner of right for ever, without any exception or impediment whatsoever.

But that abuses and frauds may be avoided by importing any kind of goods, the Catholic King wills, and takes it to be understood, that the above-named propriety be yielded to Great Britain without any territorial jurisdiction, and without any open communication by land with the country round about.

Yet whereas the communication by sea with the coast of Spain may not at all times be safe or open, and thereby it may happen that the garrison, and other inhabitants of Gibraltar may be brought to great straits; and as it is the intention of the Catholic King, only that fraudulent importations of goods should, as is above said, be hindered by an inland communication, it is therefore provided that in such cases it may be lawful to purchase, for ready money, in the neighbouring territories of Spain, provisions, and other things necessary for the use of the garrison, the inhabitants and the ships which lie in the harbour.

But if any goods be found imported by Gibraltar, either by way of barter for purchasing provisions, or under any other pretence, the same shall be confiscated, and complaint being made thereof, those persons who have acted contrary to the faith of this Treaty shall be severely punished.

And Her Britannic Majesty, at the request of the Catholic King, does consent and agree that no leave shall be given under any pretence whatsoever, either to Jews or Moors, to reside or have their dwellings in the said town of Gibraltar....

...And in case it shall hereafter seem meet to the Crown of Great Britain to grant, sell, or by any means to alienate therefrom the propriety of the said town of Gibraltar, it is hereby agreed and concluded, that preference of having the same shall always be given to the Crown of Spain, before any others.

Several of these clauses were to be the cause of friction between Britain and Spain over the following years, but the fact remained that from 1713 Gibraltar was British "for ever."

The exodus in 1704, a bas-relief in the Casa Capitular, San Roque

No matter what the treaty stated, the Spaniards considered the loss of El Peñon to be a temporary setback and George I, who came to the British throne in 1714, was at first in favour of surrendering the Rock. Britain, meanwhile, joined its former enemy France, with the Netherlands, to make the Triple Alliance, which became quadruple in 1718 when Emperor Charles, the failed Carlos III in whose name Rooke had seized the Rock, joined.

By 1720 the Earl of Stanhope, a Minister in the British Parliament, had paved the diplomatic way for returning the Rock, and George I sent Felipe V two letters. The first offered to exchange Gibraltar for Florida, which Felipe declined; the second offered to restore the Rock as soon as convenient, with no conditions attached.

King George's Promise The British monarchy was by this time constitutional and there was little that King George could do personally to make the concession. But the Spanish monarchy was still absolute, and the Spaniards looked at the second letter as King George's Promise and they couldn't understand why he didn't keep it.

It was a blow to Spanish national pride which was soon to prompt the thirteenth siege, and raise the hopes of the people most affected by the English occupation. These were the people who had fled El Peñon in 1704 and who now lived in the Campo.

Holy Rock

AT THE surrender of Gibraltar the Spanish residents fled with all they could carry. Several families went to Algeciras but the majority moved only a few miles inland, to where the Gothic King Recared had built a church 1,100 years earlier, and there on a hillside they founded for themselves the new town of San Roque – Holy Rock – from where they had a commanding view over to their homes in the old town of Gibraltar.

They took with them the keys to the Landport Gates, but over the years these have been lost. They also took the royal coat of arms that Isabella had reputedly embroidered for their ancestors in 1492. Today this standard hangs in San Roque's *Sala de Actos* in the *Casa Capitular*, literally the legal chamber in the chapter house but in effect the council chamber in the town hall. The people of San Roque are still proud of their past and will show visitors the royal standard at the Alcalde's discretion.

The Sala de Actos also has an ornately carved fresco showing some of the agony the original Gibraltarians endured in their exodus.

"La Cuidad de Gibraltar en San Roque" To this day the people of the town are officially known as "the citizens of Gibraltar residing at San Roque" and their coat of arms is unchanged from the one that Isabella granted their forebears: the three-towered castle with golden key pendant, surmounted by a crown.

The staircase leading to the first floor Sala de Actos has an elegant leaded window bearing the royal coat of arms for the Rock, plus a picture of Gibraltar as seen from San Roque, and flanked by texts describing the loss of El Peñon. In English it would read:

NO SPANIARD MAY FORGET

FIRST
That Gibraltar did not surrender to the English but to the national proclamation which supported the rights of the Archduke of Austria, pretender to the Crown of Spain in the War of Succession.

SECOND

That the surrender took place in the most honourable conditions after a heroic and desperate struggle.

THIRD

That, with the English flag hoisted unexpectedly over El Peñon, the Council, the Elders, and with them the population in its entirety, departed, preferring the loss of their goods and homes to submitting themselves to the foreign yoke, and installing themselves here while remaining loyal to the belief in their eventual return.

The loss of Gibraltar is a page in the history of Spain which is at the same time glorious and lamentable.

HEREWITH A CONFIRMATION OF THE NUMBERS OPPOSING THEM

Seventy soldiers were garrisoning the Rock, as far as one can calculate; before the laying of the siege there were also 400 inhabitants. There were 100 pieces of artillery but most of them were dismantled and the others could scarcely be used for want of personnel.

The blockading squadron consisted of 61 vessels, 68 auxiliary transports, 4,104 cannon, 25,583 artillerymen and 9,000 men who came ashore, of whom 3,000 were on the isthmus.

In these circumstances the city refused several requests to surrender without a fight and resisted with epic stoicism until further opposition would have had them destroyed.

La Línea de la Concepción Spain made certain that the British could not walk the length of the isthmus. "Without any open communication by land" said the Treaty of Utrecht; the Spanish intended to see that it was so. At the extreme range of British cannon shot they built an earth bank from the Bay to the Mediterranean and called it the Line of the Beginning – La Línea de la Concepción. Beyond it, over the years, grew a town which, not surprisingly, came to take the same name.

Today the communities of San Roque and La Línea, both owing their origins to the loss of Gibraltar, are pleasant towns in the Spanish tradition, but quite different from each other. San Roque clings to the hills, with streets grinding steeply up to the cobbled square where orange trees fruit in front of the church, and with a view from the Mirador el Poeta (the Poet's Lookout Point) that includes not only El Peñon but the blue vista of Morocco stretching from Ceuta almost to Cape Spartel.

La Línea is flat, filling the broader part of the isthmus from the Bay, where there is the recent petrol refinery, to the Mediterranean, where a few fishing boats still launch from the beach each evening.

Forty years ago the Gibraltarians used to come out to La Línea at weekends to play golf and polo, but the tiny one-storey houses extended northwards on each side of Calle Gibraltar (Gibraltar Road) and claimed the site. Today these small homes are being knocked together into larger

The Arms of Gibraltar at San Roque

ones, or giving way to low-rise apartments. To the north of the town is the gently-swelling hill known to the older people in Gibaltar as The Queen of Spain's Chair, but nobody in La Línea knows it by that name. To the south, dominating the skyline, is the stark, vertical face of Wolf's Crag, the north wall of the Rock of Gibraltar, rising at this point to 1,337 feet (407 metres).

Neutral Territory Between the "line" and the north face was, by mutual accord, the neutral territory, established after the Treaty of Sevilla in 1729. Years later, Britain drew another line bisecting this no-man's-land, and built a fence: this marks the border we see today.

The Inundation The Gibraltarians, finding conditions cramped on the Rock, filled in the swampy land just north of the Moorish Castle and built a road over it; until recently it was called Inundation Road. Over the years they grazed cattle on the reclaimed land, the only cows ever to have been kept on Gibraltar, and earlier this century they also built a racecourse.

During the Second World War all this gave way to the RAF runway, built with thousands of tons of limestone dug out from deep within the Rock as ammunition dumps and water chambers were created; since the war a considerable industrial estate has grown up, overshadowed by that immense stone wall.

The Spanish kept their half of the neutral territory clear, even having their customs post on the original line at La Línea, but during the years when the frontier was closed, they moved south, building flats and finally adding the three dual-carriageways that converge at the Gibraltar gates.

Spain has also built a long, low mole out into the Bay, a few feet inside the border and parallel with it. It's called the *Muelle de San Felipe*, and its name is the only reminder of the fort of San Felipe that once stood at the Bay end of the original *línea de la concepción*.

Rock Solid

THE SPANIARDS realised the only way they could regain possession of El Peñon was by conquest and in 1720 they began preparations for another onslaught. The Marquis de Leda was gathering a fleet in the Bay under the pretence of going to relieve the Spanish garrison in Ceuta, besieged for years by the Moors.

The British saw other interpretations, called Colonel Kane over from Menorca, which Britain had occupied since the Treaty of Utrecht, and his arrival with 500 men and ample supplies settled the issue. The Marquis de Leda sailed for Ceuta.

Five years later the Emperor Charles and King Felipe of Spain, who had earlier fought for the Spanish Crown, signed the Treaty of Vienna, pledging among other issues the return of Gibraltar, and so opening the way for the thirteenth siege.

Thirteenth Siege In February of 1727 the Spanish gathered between 15,000 and 20,000 men on the isthmus (one report gives the figure precisely at 19,270) under the Conte de las Torres, against a mere 1,500 defenders serving with General Clayton.

This time, however, numbers didn't matter. This was an artillery siege, and the guns and mortars were evenly matched. The Spanish opened fire in May with 92 cannon and 72 mortars, sending 700 shot per hour into the town for 14 days. The garrison replied with 58 guns; 21 on the Grand Battery just north of Casemates Square, 23 on the North Mole, nine at Willis's and five on the remains of the Moorish Castle. Most were six pounders but a few were of half that calibre, and 23 of them were out of commission by the end of May.

The Governor, Lord Portmore, was in England at the start of this siege; this was normal at the time, with the real work being left to the deputy. Portmore came back in late May with 5,481 men and more artillery, so that by early June the British could reopen fire with 100 guns dispersed around the northern defences.

The Spanish came back to the fight with another heavy barrage which severely damaged buildings around the Villa Vieja (Old Town) in the Casemates area, but after ten days the Spanish guns were showing severe

The isthmus and La Línea from the Upper Galleries

strain, several having exploded and others running so hot they drooped at the muzzle.

The British replied and within days had demoralised the besiegers, who were staked out on the isthmus with no protection from cannon and musket shot.

Flayed for Treachery The Spaniards had little chance of taking Gibaltar in this siege since they had no ships, hence they couldn't intercept supplies, reinforcements and ammunition reaching the garrison; vessels were offloading in Rosia Bay in total safety while the battle raged only two miles away.

The only other threats to the garrison were disease and treachery, and the Spanish came close to success without realising it when several Moors and Jews banded together and planned to seize the Landport Gates and open them to the attackers. They were betrayed; the Moors were found guilty, put to death and flayed, their skins being nailed to the gates they had planned to throw open. It was a grim warning, and many slips of sun-dried human leather came back to Britain as grisly souvenirs of the incident.

The British claimed to have fired 52,950 rounds during this siege and destroyed 23 enemy mortars and 73 guns, for the loss of 360 men from all causes. The Conde de las Torres lost 1,500 men from military action and almost 5,000 from illness. Withdrawing in July he calculated that he would have needed at least 25,000 men to give him a chance of success, not counting a small fleet of warships.

Balancing the Odds At this point it is fair to look at the chances of any army, be it British, Spanish, or even Moorish, of succeeding in taking Gibraltar by siege or direct attack. The Rock has been besieged 14 times, yet it changed hands on only five occasions: in 1309 when Spain took it from the Moors; in 1333 when the Moors took it back; in 1411 when one Moorish faction took it from another; in 1462 when Spain recaptured it; and in 1704 when England seized it.

The common factor in all those successful attacks was that the defences were poor, sometimes atrociously poor. In the first, eighth and eleventh sieges there was also the element of surprise. Provided the garrison is up to strength – and this strength need be no more than a tenth of the attackers' – and is prepared, then the Rock is virtually impregnable. The defenders have the advantages of solid barricades and high vantage points for sighting the enemy and firing down on him, while the attackers have to come in flimsy vessels or creep across the isthmus, exposed all the way.

The besieged army needs to pay more attention to maintaining supplies of food, water and ammunition than it does to fighting any war,

*She is not really an ape but that **is** Algeciras in the background*

which is why a sea blockade is vital to any attacker's plans, provided he can cut off *all* supplies for as long as may be needed.

Surprise attacks have been useful. The landing party who came up the Shepherd's Path could have succeeded if its back-up had played its part. Equally, the besieged garrison may make useful surprise attacks, as we shall see.

But the greatest threats to a garrison that was up to strength and prepared for war, were beyond any commander's control. They were treachery from within, disease, or political moves far from the scene of battle.

Hardening of Attitudes Politically, this thirteenth siege injured Spain's cause by hardening the attitude of the British on the Rock. In the following months the last remaining Spaniards were sent back over the frontier and all customs that were purely Spanish were abandoned. It is from this time that English street names began replacing the Spanish ones – though the residents of Gibraltar still thought of them in Spanish, and the modern-day Gibraltarian still talks of *Calle Mayor* though the sign says *Main Street*.

The long Spanish siesta was reduced to a short, British-style midday break, and Christmas developed as the main midwinter festival on the Rock as it did in Victorian Britain, while in Spain Los Reyes (Twelfth Night) developed as the time when the children received their presents.(Santa Claus has never visited Spain; the Three Kings of Orient stand in for him on January 6).

The British also encouraged Genoese and Jewish settlers to trade on the Rock, in defiance of what had been agreed in the Treaty of Utrecht.

The Convent In Britain, Parliament and the people thought of Gibraltar as a bastion of Protestantism in a part of the world full of Catholics, conveniently ignoring the fact that most people on the Rock were Catholic. As if to reinforce that belief, several redundant religious buildings in Gibraltar were put to more mundane use. The Nunnery of Santa Clara became a barrack; the Convent of San Juan de Dios was used for storage; the Convent of the Mercenarios became the Admiral's residence; and the empty Fransiscan Convent on Main Street became the Governor's official residence, which it is to this day.

A wealthy Spaniard had founded the convent in 1482 on another site; he gave the friars money, land and masonry in return for an assured grave for himself and his family. The monks moved to Main Street – Calle Mayor – in 1521 but left with the majority of the townspeople in 1704, to go to San Roque.

Treaty of Seville Felipe V of Spain was ill, but his second wife Elizabeth (Isabella) Farnese had taken on herself the struggle to restore El Peñon to the Spanish Crown. In 1729 Britain, Spain and France signed the Treaty of Sevilla, allowing Spain to occupy Parma and Tuscany on the Italian peninsula, but ignoring the Gibraltar issue though the Treaty of Utrecht was confirmed.

But France and Spain, which had earlier jointly signed the Treaty of Vienna (pledging the return of Gibraltar) now signed the Family Compact in which the main aim again was the restoration of Gibraltar to the Spanish Cown.

At the same time, British interests were conflicting with French in Europe, and with Spanish on the high seas, particularly the Spanish Main. The result was the Seven Years' War.

Gibraltar took only a small role in this struggle. The French landed on Menorca and Admiral Byng was sent out from Britain with reinforcements. He put in at the Rock in May 1756 for provisions and the Governor, General Fowke, insisted on keeping many of the marines so that when Byng reached Menorca on May 19 he hadn't enough men to be effective. He tried engaging the French fleet off Menorca and had the advantage of the wind, yet he failed to push home his attack, claiming that one of his ships was dismasted causing all the others to back their sails to avoid a pile-up.

Next morning he decided the relief of Menorca was out of the question and he sailed back to Gibraltar.

And there, admirals Hawke and Saunders arrested him and sent him back to Britain where on December 28 he was court-martialled not for cowardice but for not having "done his utmost," and was executed by firing squad, prompting Voltaire to write his immortal words that "it is good to kill an admiral from time to time *pour encourager les autres.*"

In 1757 William Pitt the Elder, who had tried to save Byng, devised the plan of returning Gibraltar to Spain so that Spain would turn against France, drive the French out of Menorca, and return the island to Britain...but the average Briton was already seeing the Rock of Gibraltar as a symbol of British courage and strength, and Pitt dropped the idea before the people dropped him.

High Treason On the Rock the garrisoning troops sometimes saw it differently. Three years later, 730 men in two regiments planned to massacre their officers, seize the pay chests for themselves, and arrange their escape by surrendering Gibraltar to Spain from within. A quarrel in an ale-house brought the plot to light, and the ringleaders were executed.

The Treaty of Paris, signed in 1763, gave Canada to Britain, New Orleans and Louisiana to Spain, restored Menorca to Britain once more – and confirmed the Treaty of Utrecht yet again without mentioning Gibraltar. But Britain was to have a harder time in her New England colonies, leading to the American War of Independence in 1779, which Spain saw as an ideal opportunity to make yet another attempt to seize the Rock.

This was the Fourteenth Siege, and it warrants capital letters because it was to last three years seven months and twelve days and become known in history as the Great Siege.

Punta Maroqui in the background, with Africa on the skyline
View from La Línea de la Concepción

Catalan Bay and the rain catchments
The Rock dominates the frontier

General Eliott's signature

Eliott's Rock

THE FOURTEENTH SIEGE started on July 11, 1779. The Governor, General George Augustus Eliott, was nearly 62 and had been on the Rock for two years. He had maintained friendly relations with the Spanish and had paid a courtesy call on General Mendoza on June 19, his cool reception being the first hint of impending trouble.

Eliott had also built up the Rock's defences from an abysmally poor standard so that when the frontier was closed on June 21 he had 663 cannon and 5,382 men in a range of units: artillery, engineers, artificers, men from the 12th, 39th, 56th, 58th and 72nd regiments, as well as Hanoverian troops under Major-General de la Motte. Language was no problem since Eliott himself had served in the Prussian Army and spoke fluent German and French, but he was still worried about the garrison strength; he considered 7,000 troops to be the minimum to resist a siege, particularly in view of what was happening in Spain.

Alvarez and Falkenstein Across the isthmus 28,332 Spanish soldiers were massing under the command of Don Martín Alvarez de Sotomayor, joined by 33,038 French under Baron Falkenstein, giving the attackers a strength of 61,370, almost twelve to one. All were nominally under the command of the Duc de Crillon who was away in Menorca, leading the Spanish attack against the British.

This time the Spanish controlled the seas around the Rock and could apply an effective blockade most of the time, while Eliott's weak force of the 60-gun *Panther*, the 28-gun *Enterprise*, the *Childers* of 14 guns, the *Gibraltar* with 12, and the *Fortune* with 10, was commanded by Admiral Duff, who was even weaker than his fleet. Eliott ordered 900 men to leave their ships and help the soldiers on the barricades.

Duff had been refitting five warships for the King of Morocco in Gibraltar harbour, and now refused to complete the order because he needed the cordage and spars. Eliott called the British consul over from Tanger to give Duff some plain talking in priorities: without his ships, would the King of Morocco risk running the blockade to supply food to the Rock? And if not, would Duff accept responsibility for losing Gibraltar? The king got his warships.

New Jerusalem The siege started slowly as Alvarez's men concentrated on digging their defences across the line of conception and gradually working them southward. Eliott used the phoney war to tighten his defences as much as possible and to urge the 6,700 civilians on the Rock to leave. Most did, and most of those who remained built themselves a shanty town on the Windmill Flats down by Europa; among the names they found for it were New Jerusalem and Black Town, preferring them to the Spanish name of Tarfes Altos for the area in general. But a few people decided to stay in the Old Town, and were to be the cause of trouble later.

"Britons, Strike Home!" With still no shot fired from land by either side, Eliott decided the waiting was over. On September 12 he invited Mrs Skinner, wife of an officer in the Soldier Artificer Company (the company had been founded on the Rock in 1772 and was a forerunner of the Royal Engineers), to put a lighted taper to a loaded and primed cannon. Eliott shouted "Britons, strike home!" and the bombardment began. The next day, with Alvarez's troops reluctant to waste their powder in reply, Eliott hosted the annual American Gentlemen's Dinner, toasting the men who had been on the Heights of Abraham in Quebec 20 years earlier, to the day.

After that the belt-tightening began in earnest. There was no food for the civil population who had to make what arrangements they could, or starve. Later in the siege Eliott himself lived for a week on four ounces of rice a day to show his men it could be done, but they merely commented he was a vegetarian to begin with.

Boredom and hunger were relieved on January 19, 1780, when Admiral Sir George Rodney's fleet – including the ship of the line *Victory* which was later to fly Nelson's flag – having avoided the French at Brest and defeated the Spanish off Cape St Vincent, sailed into harbour with ample stores, plus troops of the 73rd Highlanders on their way to Menorca, though some historians say they were going to the West Indies. Eliott did to Rodney what had once been done to Byng; he commandeered the troops and sent only Admiral Duff in their place.

Lieutenant Shrapnel With bellies once again full, Eliott's men could tackle one of the problems that had emerged from that first bombardment. Solid cannonball shot was gradually giving way to hollowed-out balls, known aptly as shells, and filled with explosives. Shot was useless on the isthmus unless it scored a direct hit, and shell was little better since the sand muffled the explosion. Captain Mercier came forward with the suggestion of shorter fuses so the shell could explode in the air over the enemy lines, and later in the siege Lieutenant Shrapnel, serving with the Hanoverians, devised a shell that burst into horrifying, jagged pieces. His invention has immortalied his name but has killed thousands of people in the wars since.

Depression Carriage Lieutenant G. F. Köhler of the Royal Artillery made less of a name for himself when he invented the depression carriage, a heavy wooden chassis on which the mounted cannon could be tilted to fire downwards. The need arose because the ever-encroaching

The town and harbour from the Upper Rock; refinery is in La Línea

Spanish trenches had come so close to the north cliff of the Rock that conventional cannon, particularly when mounted high on the bastions, fired over the enemy troops' heads.

Köhler had to find a way of preventing the shell rolling out of the gunbarrel, and he needed to rope down the entire weapon so it didn't rebound into the air after each firing, but the invention went into service in February 1782, and a full-scale model now stands outside the Health Centre on Casemates Square.

But back to the Great Siege. 1780 was a quiet year on the Rock. Few shots were fired by either side and the main problem was disease. Scurvy ravaged Eliott's troops until he seized the lemons aboard a Dutch freighter that put into the harbour, and mixed their juice with brandy. Smallpox was killing the children, but Eliott's policy here was to let nature take its course and if that resulted in fewer mouths to feed, maybe that wasn't so bad in the circumstances.

Fireships On June 7 the Spanish tried the old tactic of sending in fireships, and would have succeeded in penetrating the harbour with their nine vessels but for a sudden change in the wind. After that they brought out gunboats, low craft 60 feet (20 metres) long, relying mainly on oarsmen who lined up the 26-pound cannon on a fixed mounting in the bows.

These ships came and went regardless of tides or winds and their crews soon found they could attack at night as well as by day. Eliott had no defence against them beyond ordering a total blackout, and they remained an irritation to him, like buzzing hornets, for the remainder of the siege.

The Great Siege of Gibraltar was already becoming one of the talking points of Europe, particularly.when Morocco declared war on Britain and leased Tetuan and Tanger to Spain. In diplomatic circles Britain and Spain had almost struck a bargain with the return of the Rock as the main prize, but when the Gordon Riots broke out in Britain, Spain reduced her offer, thinking it only a matter of time before El Peñon fell.

It didn't fall. And when the second supply convoy reached the Rock on April 12, 1781, everybody could see that it wouldn't fall. For weeks the garrison and townspeople had been so hungry they were scavenging the Upper Rock and the shoreline for anything edible, from wild onions to seaweed, and now that relief had come surrender was unthinkable. So even as Admiral Derby was discharging his cargo the Spanish opened fire from 170 guns and 80 mortars, and in six weeks lobbed 56,000 shot and 20,000 shell into the town.

Seventy soldiers were killed in the barrage, but that was insignificant compared with the stocks of hoarded food that were exposed in basements and back rooms as the enemy artillery destroyed many of the

St Michael's Road leads to the highest point; Spain in background

houses in the Old Town. The troops rioted, plundered the area and gorged themselves on what they found, while their officers stood back. A few days later Eliott appointed a Provost Marshal who hanged a few of the looters and so managed to restore order, just short of a mutiny.

The Great Sortie The best way to boost morale is to take the initiative. Eliott had been watching the steady advance of the Spanish trenches along the sandy isthmus, listening to the reports of the few deserters who made their way onto the Rock, and he decided that early on November 27, 1781, he would counter-attack. With no warning to anybody, Eliott ordered 103 officers and 2,065 men of the 72nd Regiment to parade on the Red Sands (now the Alameda Gardens area) just after midnight. Then, nominally under the command of Brigadier-General Ross but with Eliott unable to keep away, the party filed out through Landport Gate under the setting moon and at 2.45am attacked the Spanish defences.

Eliott had caught the enemy totally unprepared with few soldiers on duty. The men of the 72nd spiked ten 13-inch mortars and eighteen 26-pound guns, set fire to the wooden superstructure of the trenches, and destroyed several magazines of ammunition.

In the noise and smoke about 40 Spanish cavalrymen came out to attack but on seeing such superior forces hurried back as fast as their mounts could carry them.

The British lost five men, with 25 wounded – and a lone Highlander of the 73rd Regiment lost his kilt. The Garrison Orders recorded the great sortie in stirring sentiment: "The bravery and conduct of the whole detachment, officers, seamen and soldiers on this glorious occasion surpasses the Governor's utmost acknowledgements."

And as soon as the Spanish and French had rebuilt their advance trenches, Eliott's ageing deputy, Lieutenant-General Boyd, reaped some glory by setting fire to them a second time, using red-hot cannonballs.

Scurvy Disease became Eliott's greatest worry as the blockade dragged interminably on. Scurvy racked the defenders, with up to 500 of them in hospital at any time; and when the 97th Regiment reached the Rock in March 1782 a hundred of its soldiers were so ill with scurvy they went straight into hospital.

Eliott then made a deal with the captain of the *Mercury*, which was slipping out of harbour for a run back to England with a number of half-starved passengers. The ship's secret orders called for it to put into Lisbon, load up with lemons, and return to the Rock: the passengers ignored the hint to trans-ship in Portugal and were chagrined to find themselves back at the besieged Rock.

Chevalier d'Arcon By now there was scarcely any literate person in Europe who had not heard of the Great Siege of Gibraltar. The Duc de Crillon, having driven the British out of Menorca, now came back to lead the final assault – as he thought – on Gibraltar. His problem was that King Carlos III had offered a reward to anybody who could unseat Eliott and his gang, and the Chevalier d'Arcon's idea of using floating castles had been accepted.

If d'Arcon's idea worked, of course, he would get the credit. If it did not, Crillon may well get the blame, unless he prepared his defence carefully. And at first glance the floating batteries seemed as if they might succeed, for d'Arcon had taken ten ships of from 600 to 1,400 tons burden, stripped them of their superstructure and, using 200,000 cubic feet (6,000 cubic metres) of timber had rebuilt them as floating castles.

Floating batteries The specifications were astonishing. Each ship had a three-foot (one metre) thick sandwich of wood, wet sand, wood, wet cork, and wood again, as defence against fire and splinter; overhead was a roof of rope net and rawhide, with absolutely everything protected by a sprinkler system from a water tank on the mast.

Each of these incredible ships carried from eight to twenty brass cannon, according to the vessel's size, with crews varying from 250 to 760. In total there were 138 guns and 5,190 men.

That was just for the sea attack. Meanwhile, d'Arcon's land batteries were massing; a further 246 guns and mortars and an army of 40,000 men, whom the Duc de Crillon found himself commanding.

There was no way that this party could be hidden. Indeed, Carlos III wanted the entire civilized world to witness the recapture of Gibraltar. Legend adds the pleasing little story of the Queen of Spain who was so convinced of success that she invited her own retinue along and established them with her on top of that little hill just to the north of La Línea de la Concepción which a few Gibraltarians still know as the Queen of Spain's Chair. She vowed (says the legend) that she would stay there until she saw the flag of Spain flying once more over the parapets of her beloved Gibraltar.

Sergeant-Major Ince Meanwhile, Eliott was desperately searching for a way to get a cannon up onto the Notch, a belly-button pimple in the North Face 800 feet (250 metres) above the isthmus. Sergeant-Major Ince of the Military Artificers suggested he could drive a tunnel through 500 feet (150 m) of solid rock with the help of every miner in the garrison.

In five weeks, 13 men cut a tunnel eight feet (2.4m) square 82 feet (25m) into the limestone, a fact which is recorded on a plaque at the entrance to Ince's tunnel. Another plaque inside contrasts this achievement, excellent though it was, with the efforts of a fully-mechanised Tunnelling Company of the Royal Engineers who drilled a shaft 14 feet (4.25 m) square for 180 feet (55m) in a week during the Second World War.

Tunnelling Ince and his party drilled pilot holes in the rock with a cylindrical rod around a yard (metre) long and 1.5 inches (4cm) thick, tapering to a single cutting edge at the business end. One man, sometimes two, sledge-hammered the other end of the rod while another man steadied it in his hands, turning the cutting edge a few degrees after every hammer-blow. When there were several of these shafts, each around two feet (60cm) long cut into the advancing face of the tunnel, the miners rammed home their gunpowder and blasted their way a few feet further.

Changing the Guard outside the Convent

Camp Bay and Little Bay

Europa Point and its lighthouse

The old church of San Roque

The fumes from these detonations nearly reached choking point, forcing the miners to cut their way through the side of the tunnel to find fresh air – and discover they had made a perfect emplacement for one of Lt Köhler's depression guns, before reaching the Notch.

Upper Galleries The tunnelling continued, with three more gun ports being opened before the Great Siege ended. But Ince didn't stop even then; he drove his Windsor Gallery (now called the Upper Gallery for reasons that are imminently obvious) a total of 370 feet (113m) across the North Face and eventually pierced the crust of the East Face, affording a spectacular view of the rain catchments and Catalan Bay. After that he carved the King's and the Queen's Lines, but these "lower galleries" are not open to the modern visitor.

While Ince and his immediate superior, Lt Evelegh of the Corps of Engineers, were engrossed high on the Rock, the Chevalier d'Arcon was continuing work on the floating batteries at Algeciras as soldiers and sailors arrived by the thousand, until 14 admirals were flying their flags in the Bay.

The word had gone out all over Europe that the grand attack would begin on August 25, allowing everybody who was anybody to reach the Campo de Gibraltar in time to see history being made.

Royal Audience The Compte d'Artois, brother of Louis XVI, was there; so was his cousin the Duc de Bourbon, and the Prince of Nassau. And, of course, if legend is to be believed, the Queen of Spain was at her hilltop vantage point behind La Línea...

If Her Majesty had night vision her spectacular viewpoint would have allowed her to witness the army's preparations on the night of August 15-16 as 15,000 labourers filed through the Spanish lines and during the hours of darkness built a wall right across the isthmus almost where the frontier is today. Using half a million sandbags, dropped at the rate of 20 a second, they threw up a pallisade nine feet (3m) high and ten feet (3.5m) wide.

At the same time they dumped down barrels filled with sand to build another wall, six feet (2m) high, stretching back beyond the "line of conception" to protect the 10,000 soldiers who then filed out and took up their positions at this new defensive line.

And Eliott, though fully aware of what was happening, ordered that not a shot be fired.

Delays The August 25 deadline passed with no attack as Crillon still tried to have the entire scenario cancelled; but as insurance against its failure if it went ahead he wrote scores of letters criticising d'Arcon's planning. But the king decreed that preparations had gone too far and that the attack was to proceed.

Red-hot shot On September 8 the British bombarded the new Spanish lines with red-hot shot, some of it coming from Ince's Windsor Gallery. There was carnage among the Spanish soldiers, with heavy losses as they pulled back to the safety of the original lines. If the Queen of Spain really was on top of the Queen of Spain's Chair, she must have been appalled.

For the next three days the Duc de Crillon fired on the Rock with 170 guns from the isthmus, sending 4,000 shot and shell into Gibraltar town in a continuous barrage. On September 10, Admiral Córdoba's fleet added its broadsides to the daïly ration of shot coming from the isthmus, and on the twelfth the remainder of the fleets of France and Spain sailed into the Bay, bringing seven three-deckers, 31 two-deckers, three frigates and six smaller vessels.

Now at last the Chevalier d'Arcon was ready for what could be the greatest day in the history of Spain since Ferdinand and Isabella drove the Moors from Granada in 1492. Indeed, Crillon had given d'Arcon the ultimatum of attacking on this day or not at all.

Final assault At dawn on September 13 the final assault began. On the sea, the ten floating batteries sailed slowly out of Algeciras, their reluctant crews having been marched aboard at bayonet-point. On the land, 40,000 soldiers waited for the defeat of Gibraltar and the order to storm its northern defences and recapture it for the Spanish Crown. And, according to that legend, the Queen of Spain saw it all from the top of her hill.

The floating batteries slowly crossed the Bay, with the Chevalier d'Arcon, aboard *Talla Piedra* (the name loosely means "stature of granite"), surging ahead to show the way around a treacherous middle-ground sandbank. Rear-admiral Moreno, aboard *Pastora*, thought

"Shot and Shell" in the Upper Galleries

d'Arcon was trying to steal his glory and stuck close to the chevalier's ship.

Sandbank These were therefore the only two of the grand, impregnable, unsinkable, floating batteries to get close enough to the Rock to be effective. Of the other eight, several stuck on the sandbank, others dropped anchor too far from shore, and some came up opposite Rosia and Little bays where there was nothing worth attacking.

Crillon's inherited land-and-sea armada had a potential of 466 guns: the 138 aboard the floating batteries, though most of those were now out of range; 186 on the isthmus; and 142 aboard the conventional warships which still rode at anchor on the other side of the Bay.

Against them Eliott had a mere 96 guns, but he opened fire as soon as he could. At first the British artillerymen were using cold cannonballs but in the early afternoon the furnaces were fiery enough for red-hot shot to be hurled against *Talla Piedra* and *Pastora*. Soon smoke began rising from d'Arcon's ship and though her crew fought back with the sprinkler system the flames took hold and by early evening her captain, the Prince of Nassau, ordered his gunpowder to be dampened to avoid an explosion. He then took *Talla Piedra*'s only boat and rowed himself ashore.

Disaster By now everybody realised the attack was a disaster. On the Spanish side, only the Duc de Crillon was pleased; he had prophesied failure and now he could take advantage of it by ordering all the remaining floating batteries to be evacuated and burned where they lay.

But there were not enough boats to take off all the crews. While d'Arcon tried to get the order countermanded, Crillon's men put torches to the ships, many still with their crews aboard.

The British gunners opened up on these targets lighting the night sky until Captain Curtis, RN, ordered a cease-fire and led a small-boat party to rescue the Spanish crewmen.

He saved 357 before being driven back by the searing heat, and when dawn came the watchers from Algeciras to the line of conception saw the dismal sight of smoking hulks and floating corpses. On that sad day of September 13, Spain had lost 1,473 men killed from the floating batteries, not counting Crillon's prisoners, and a score or so more victims of other actions. The garrison lost one officr and 15 men killed, and five officers and 63 men injured.

Queen of Spain It was obviously the end of the Great Siege. The troops were disbanded; the Compte d'Artois, the Duc de Bourbon and the Prince of Nassau went their way, as did the thousands of other spectators. But – according to tradition – the Queen of Spain was still there on her hilltop, where she had vowed to remain until she saw the flag of Spain fly over the battlements of Gibraltar. The legend claims that Eliott heard of her plight, arranged for the flag to be waved, and the Queen retired in dignity.

The legend, not surprisingly, is unknown in Spain, and the hill behind La Línea does not have any notable Spanish name.

Peace negotiations began in Paris, but life on the Rock continued as before, with the British defenders once more facing starvation. Then on October 10, 1782, Lord Howe's fleet of 34 warships arrived in the strait escorting 31 merchantmen. Strong currents and winds kept them out of the Bay and they hove to off Marbella on the Costa del Sol. Eighty French and Spanish ships left Algeciras in pursuit but Howe slipped south, via Tetuan, and reached Gibraltar in safety.

He brought the 25th and 59th infantry regiments, totalling 1,600 men; he also landed much-needed food – and venereal disease to go with the outbreak of rabies among the Rock's few remaining dogs.

Treaty of Versailles In the closing weeks of hostilities Crillon tried to find a tunnel that had been started in the previous siege of 1727; he had the idea of blasting down the entire North Face of the Rock. But nobody had any heart for another major enterprise and on February 2, 1783, the Spanish soldiers heard that peace had been signed on January 20 with the Treaty of Versailles, and they shouted the news to the British. The Great Siege ended officially on March 12, 1783.

When they balanced the books, the British reckoned that the Gibraltar garrison lost 333 men killed or died of wounds; 536 died of sickness; 181 discharged due to incurable illness during the siege; 138 discharged with war wounds; and 43 deserted. The total: 1,231.

The British fired 205,328 rounds of shot and shell, which if accurate shows a remarkable standard of quartermastering, using 8,000 barrels of powder in the process. Fifty-three cannon were put out of action.

The Spanish accounts showed aroud 6,000 men killed in action or dying of wounds, with 258,837 shot and shell being fired, another remarkably accurate figure.

General Eliott and the Duc de Crillon examined each other's defences afterwards and Crillon commented that Ince's galleries were "works worthy of the Romans."

Eliott left the Rock to receive the thanks of Parliament, the Order of the Bath, a pension of £1,500 a year, and in 1787 elevation to the peerage as Baron Heathfield. He died in 1795 and is buried in Holy Trinity Church, Colchester.

St George's Hall in the Upper Galleries

Nelson's Rock

BETWEEN 1793 and 1805 Britain and France were in conflict as Napoleon Bonaparte sought to build an empire on land, while Britain was beginning to build one along its sea routes.

And Spain was once again in turmoil. With much of her territory overrun by French troops, the garrison forces on the Rock crossed the frontier to help Spanish patriots seize Tarifa from the French, and later helped them take Ceuta, in Morocco. And when the French attacked San Roque, the inhabitants fled into the fortress of Gibraltar for protection – the town their ancestors had quit under duress in 1704.

It was at this time that, quite quietly, the Spaniards razed their forts of San Felipe and Santa Barbara, at opposite ends of the original "line of conception."

In 1802 the Rock had one of its least popular governors, and its only one from the Royal Family. The Duke of Kent, fourth son of George III and later to be Queen Victoria's father, was so strict in suppressing drunkenness that he nearly started a mutiny at Christmas, and he was hastily recalled.

During the Napoleonic Wars, the strategies of the Great Siege of Gibraltar had given way to the great sieges of the sea, and from May 1803 to March 1805 Horatio Nelson had been in command of the Mediterranean fleet, almost totally occupied with blockading part of the French navy in the port of Toulon.

But on March 31 as some of Nelson's ships were away seeking onions and lemons, the preventors of scurvy, 11 French ships slipped harbour under Vice-Admiral Villeneuve and escaped to Cádiz where they joined the Spanish fleet.

Villeneuve's orders were to sail to the West Indies to draw away the British blockading squadrons and so leave Bonaparte free to invade Britain; he had 2,000 small boats and 90,000 troops waiting in France and needed just four days without British interference in the Channel.

Nelson followed Villeneuve to the West Indies and back, always about four days behind. But as the French admiral swung north for Biscay on his final run home, Nelson turned to the south and put in at Gibraltar.

El Ferrol While he was waiting under the shadow of the Rock he learned that Villeneuve's latest orders were sending him to the Spanish port of El Ferrol, later to be the birthplace of General Franco.

Nelson sailed from Gibraltar, had a brief encounger off Finisterre – winds were too light for a full-scale battle – and came back to Britain while the Allied fleet went to Vigo. There Villeneuve was to receive yet more orders, virtually giving him the option of going to the Netherlands via the north of Scotland, or back to Cádiz. He chose the latter.

Nelson was recalled from his leave with his wife Emma and daughter Horatia, and as he sailed aboard *Victory* from Portsmouth on September 15 1805, he wrote to a friend of the battle that was to come, though nobody knew it was to be off Spain's Cape Trafalgar.

"My shattered frame, if I survive that day, will require rest, and that is all I shall ask for. If I fail on such a glorious occasion, it shall be my pride to take care that my friends shall not blush for me – these things are in the hand of a wise and just Providence, and his will be done."

Cádiz Rally Nelson and his fleet rallied off Cádiz where Nelson planned his strategy for the coming encounter...if the enemy ever left the shelter of Cádiz harbour.

"I shall go at them at once if I can – about one third of their line from their leading ship. It will bring forward a pell-mell battle, and that is what I want."

Vice-Admiral Villeneuve had heard that Bonaparte planned to replace him if he stayed any longer in port, so on October 19, with the wind in the north-east, he set sail, his 33 ships outnumbering the 27 waiting for him over the horizon.

Captain Blackwood, on patrol aboard the frigate *Euryalus* with a small squadron, saw the enemy topsails being set, ordered one of his frigates

The Catholic cathedral

53

back to Nelson with the news and another to Gibraltar to recall the six ships provisioning there. Then he shadowed the Allied fleet for 18 hours until Nelson could come in close and position himself during the night of 20-21 October.

Vice-Admiral Collingwood, Nelson's next-in-command, aboard *Royal Sovereign*, described the action in despatches:

At daylight, when Cape Trafalgar bore E by S about seven leagues, the enemy was discovered six or seven miles to the eastward, the wind about west and very light...

The Spaniards, under the direction of Gravina, wore with their heads to the northwards and formed a crescent convexing to leeward...

As the mode of attack had been previously determined, few signals were necessary and none was made...

Aboard *Victory*, Nelson wore his full-dress uniform with all his orders and decorations as he brought his will up to date, remembering both his mistress Lady Hamilton, and his wife Emma. And as Collingwood's ship came within range Nelson ordered one of the few signals of the day, but it was to be the most famous of his career.

"England Expects..." "Suppose we telegraph 'Nelson confides that every man will do his duty'?" he asked, but the flag commander suggested that for brevity they signal *England expects that every man will do his duty.*

"That will do," said Nelson. "Make it directly." Shortly after, as Captain Blackwood took his leave after reporting for orders, Nelson had a premonition of death. "God bless you, Blackwood. I shall never see you again."

Collingwood's dispatches take up the story: *The action began at twelve o'clock...the enemy's ships fought with a gallantry highly honourable (but) about three p.m. many of them having struck their colours, their line gave way...*

Victory came up alongside the French ship *Rédoutable* and a marksman in the rigging shot Nelson in the left shoulder.

Two of his crew having lifted him up (wrote Collingwood) , *he exclaimed "They have done for me at last; my back-bone is shot through." On being told that the surgeon was about to examine his wound he said: "It is of no use; he can do nothing for me, he had better attend to the others." He then eagerly inquired how the day was going; and when informed that none of his ships had struck, he said: "I am a dead man; I am going fast; let my dear Lady Hamilton have my hair, and all other things belonging to me..."*

He spoke of his interment, and desired to be buried by the side of his parents, unless the King should order diffrerently. He then kept on repeating "Thank God I have done my duty!" and...he expired at a quarter past four o'clock in the afternoon.

Lieutenant Köhler's depression carriage

Collingwood didn't mention the disputed phrase "Kiss me, Hardy!," but other witnesses claim Nelson asked it of Hardy as a mark of friendship and farewell.

On the broad scale, the Battle of Trafalgar was a triumph for the British Navy in destroying the Allied fleet, but for several months Bonaparte retained his threat to invade Britain. On the narrow scale, Trafalgar was carnage: 2,330 Allied sailors were killed or wounded and 20 of their 33 ships struck their colours, but bad weather prevented Collingwood's damaged fleet from taking more than four into Gibraltar harbour as prizes.

Trafalgar Cemetery The British fleet was badly mauled and 1,214 men were killed or wounded, two of them being buried in the tiny plot just outside Gibraltar's Southport Gates, which is known today as the Trafalgar Cemetery.

Nelson's body was preserved in a barrel of brandy and was landed at Rosia Bay while Collingwood prepared his fleet for the long journey home to England.

Nelson never had his wish to be buried beside his parents, and his remains now lie in the crypt of St Paul's. A grateful Government gave his two sisters £10,000 each; his elder brother received an earldom, an income of £6,000 a year, and £100,000 to buy an estate. The greatest honour the Government could give Nelson was to put his statue on top of a tall column in a London square that was renamed Trafalgar.

And Gibraltar received its recognition as a vital garrison and staging post in the growing British Empire. As sail gave way to steam and the Suez Canal provided a short sea route to the Orient, Gibraltar – and Malta – became vital to Britain as it expanded to become, for a short while, the world's leading industrial and trading nation.

THE HITLER WAR, 1939 – 1945

WHEN France fell and the German Army was at the base of the Pyrenees, the future for Gibraltar suddenly looked bleak. German and Italian troops had helped General Fransisco Franco to power as Spanish dictator, and Hitler now asked him for permission to come back, cross the country, and seize Gibraltar.

Franco refused. If Hitler won the war, he'd be there to stay; if he lost, Spain would be at odds with the victors.

Meanwhile, 14,000 Gibraltarians had been evacuated from the Rock as a precaution. Those who had gone to French Morocco had to be brought back when France collapsed; they stayed for a few days on the Rock then came to Britain for the remainder of the war, many of them being put up in hotels in London during the worst of the Blitz before moving on to peace in Northern Ireland. The fortunate few were those evacuated to Jamaica, who enjoyed idyllic weather, never saw an air raid, and were the first to come home in 1945.

The 4,000 essential workers who stayed on saw few air raids, the worst being on 24-25 September, 1940, when up to 200 French planes attacked from Morocco, as retribution for Britain's sinking of the French fleet in Oran.

The greatest impact on Gibraltar by far was the several miles of tunnels cut deep inside the limestone by Army engineers, dwarfing the passages that Sergeant Major Ince and his crew had carved during the Great Siege. One such highway running the length of the Rock is called the Great North Road, and leading off it are chambers for barracking several thousand troops, for providing hospitals, vehicle stores, food stores, and ammunition dumps – but not one of them is open to the public even 40 years after the war.

Around 1,750,000 tons of rock were hewn in the process, most of it being used as foundations for the runway of Royal Air Force Gibraltar as it extended into the Bay; it had already flattened the racecourse and the football pitch.

Gibraltar was vital for the British war effort, particularly in servicing convoys into and out of the western Mediterranean. Without Gib it's doubtful if Britain could have managed to maintain the fragile supply line to Malta, and without both fortresses, the invasion of North Africa in November 1942, Operation Torch, would have been far more difficult.

Spain helped guarantee Torch's success by following Nelson's example and turning a blind eye on what it didn't want to see. Hundreds of Spanish workers came over daily from La Línea, passing the great build-up of aircraft, tanks and ships, some of which were even anchored in Spanish territorial waters, yet not a hint of it appears to have reached Germany.

It wasn't for lack of power that Hitler let Operation Torch continue; his forces had already sunk *Ark Royal* within sight of the Rock, they continued to attack the Malta convoys, and they were active in the strait until Germany surrendered in May 1945.

On The Rock

THE TOWN

GIBRALTAR is full of history, as a journey from Landport Gate to Europa Point, and then onto the Upper Rock, will reveal.

Landport Gate General Eliott led his troops out through Landport Gate to attack the Spanish positions during the Great Siege. From Casemates Square you can still trace something of the route he took, though many of the details have changed. A tunnel leads through the Grand Battery, built on the site of the original Moorish wall and incorporating much of its structure, and opens onto what, in Eliott's time, was a drawbridge over a defensive ditch which drained into the old Inundation.

Today the ditch has gone, the Inundation itself is lost under the foundations of Glacis Road – formerly Inundation Road – and the drawbridge has given way to a sedate footbridge leading down to Smith-Dorrien Avenue.

Casemates Gates There are two other ways out of Casemates Square. At the north-west corner, beyond the reconstruction of Lieutenant Kohler's depression carriage, are Casemate Gates, a double-arched exit for vehicles on the site of the old Moorish Water Gate, for in the early days the waters of the Bay came right up to here.

The original arch of Casemates Gates was built in 1824 when Gibraltar's governor was the Second Earl of Chatham, brother of William Pitt. The second arch was opened in 1884 by the governor of the day, Lieutenant-General Sir John Adye, while the older of the pedestrian-only arches dates from 1859. Casemates Gates not only serve as the prime access to the Town from Waterport, they also carry the overhead section of Smith-Dorrien Avenue bringing traffic from Spain.

Ceremony of the Keys Casemates is also the setting for the once-yearly Ceremony of the Keys, marking what was, until early this century, the nightly performance of locking up the fortress between dusk and daybreak; one of the governors used to sleep with the enormous Gibraltar key tucked under his pillow.

For as long as this nightly ritual endured, soldiers marched the streets at all hours, challenging each other and shouting their responses. William Makepeace Thackeray described the scene in 1844: "...and not here in

Commercial (Casemates) *Square alone, but all over the huge rock in the darkness, all through the mysterious zigzags, round the dark cannon-ball pyramids...poor fellows are marching and clapping muskets and crying "All's Well"...*

For the modern visitor the other way out of Casemates Square is to the south – straight into Main Street with its problems of one-way traffic in certain stretches at certain times on certain days. It is here that the British influence of Gibraltar is at its strongest, with British goods in British-style shops, even though many of them trade under Spanish names.

Post Office The Post Office, midway down on the right, is undoubtedly British in style. It opened in September 1858, selling British stamps with a Gibraltar overprint until the Rock had its own issue on New Year's Day 1886. The first pictorial definitives came out in 1931, with commemoratives hitting the market in 1935.

House of Assembly Further down Main Street a smart white building stands slightly back from the pavement, allowing postcard and ice cream sellers to pitch under two trees. The building began life as the Exchange and Commercial Library in 1817 but on 23 November 1950 it became the home of the new Legislative Council, inaugurated by the Duke of Edinburgh. The LegCo had four official, seven elected and two nominated members, but on 26 August 1969 it gave way to the present House of Assembly, which has a Speaker and 15 elected members, plus the Attorney General and the Financial and Development Secretary.

Five of those elected members form the Council of Ministers which is the effective Government for domestic matters, with Britain retaining responsibility for defence and external affairs. There is, for example, no such person as the Ambassador for Gibraltar any more than there are ambassadors or consuls for the Isle of Man or the Channel Islands, though all three territories accept consuls from other countries: the Israeli Consulate, as an example, is on the opposite side of Main Street.

The Gibraltar Government has a series of ministries, some of them seemingly a strange mixture of interests: Economic Development and Trade; Public Works; Tourism and Postal Services; Housing and Sport; Education, Labour and Social Security; Municipal Services; Medical and Health Services; and the Treasury – but their offices are scattered around the town.

Police Behind the House of Assembly is John Mackintosh Square, named from a local benefactor, and beside that is the Piazza; north from here, running parallel to Main Street, is the narrowish street known as Irish Town holding several consulates, a fish and chip shop, and the Police headquarters: on the Rock it's an *Office*, not a *Station*. The Gib Police was founded in 1829, only weeks after the setting up of the Metropolitan Police in London, making it the second oldest force in the Commonwealth. With around 200 officers it's also among the Commonwealth's smallest forces.

Catholic Cathedral Back along Main Street a hundred yards south of the House of Assembly stands the Catholic Cathedral of St Mary the Crowned, built by the Moors as a mosque in the thirteenth century, converted to a church by the Spanish in 1462, and raised to the status of a cathedral in 1841.

A tradition claims that Their Catholic Majesties Ferdinand and Isabella ordered the place to be rebuilt in 1502, but little happened beyond the erection of a belfry with a clock on it, and the carving of the Royal arms on the north gate; the carving has now been included in the wall of a tiny courtyard beside the cathedral in what remains of the large Moorish orange grove.

There was more work done in 1550, but during the Great Siege of 1779-83 the church was such a landmark that it was severely damaged. Rebuilding began in 1787, with the tower being added in 1820 and capped in 1874.

The Bedenham Affair On 27 April 1951 several stained glass windows were destroyed in the cathedral and the town suffered widespread but superficial damage when the motor vessel *Bedenham* blew up in the harbour with her cargo of explosives. Part of the ship was hurled right over the Rock and came down in the sea at Catalan Bay. Thirteen people died and scores were injured, and the Spanish rushed in doctors from La Línea de la Concepción to help.

Anglican Cathedral Little more than a hundred yards further down Main Street the Anglican Cathedral of the Holy Trinity stands on an island site to the right. The governor of the day, Lord Chatham, laid the foundation stone in June 1825, and Queen Adelaide attended its consecration as a church in October 1838; the building had seen temporary use as a hospital in 1837. In 1841 it became a cathedral with a diocese covering southern Europe and extending into north Africa, but in 1979 the boundaries changed and for Anglicans it is now the Cathedral of the Diocese of Gibraltar in Europe, covering the entire continent outside

The Anglican cathedral

the British Isles. Built in an arabesque style which suits the location, the cathedral was another of the casualties of the *Bedenham* disaster.

From here we can make a short detour north up Bomb House Lane to the original eighteenth-century bomb house, now the Gibraltar Museum and custodian of some of the best Moorish baths in Europe as well as a replica of the Gibraltar skull and a large model of the Rock in the nineteenth century; or we can go on south, down Secretary's Lane and Governor's Lane,to pick up Main Street at Convent Place.

The Convent As the official residence of the Governor, the Convent is *not* open to the public. You will not, therefore, see the nave of the old chapel, now converted into a ballroom, nor will you see the ornamental panels tracing the story of Gibraltar through its rulers, from Tarik ibn Zeyad to modern times.

Panels in some of the doors are recycled from tables aboard the floating batteries that the Chevalier d'Arcon launched against the Rock in 1782, and in the courtyard stands a large wooden statue of General Eliott holding the keys to the city: this was carved from the bowsprit of the Spanish man-of-war *San Juan*, captured at Trafalgar.

There is also a large dragon tree, *dracaena draco*, which some authorities estimate to be 1,500 years old: at its youngest it's certainly seen over a thousand summers.

Changing the Guard Each Tuesday at 10.20am precisely the ceremony of the Changing of the Guard fills Convent Place and draws visitors in their hundreds. It is the only regular military pageant left on the Rock following the withdrawal, on 31 July 1986, of the ceremonial guard at the frontier gates with the lowering of the Union flag at sunset.

King's Chapel King's Chapel, the garrison church beside the Convent (it was Queen's Chapel during Victorian times, but Queen Elizabeth didn't want to change the name again), *is* open to the public. Inside, under the ceremonial colours of several British regiments, lie the remains of the wife of the Spanish governor of 1648 (*not* the wife of the Spaniard who financed the original Fransiscan Convent in 1482; she's in unhallowed ground somewhere else) and the British governors O'Hara and Campbell, buried in 1802 and 1813.

Supreme Court Roughly diagonally opposite is the Supreme Court, not open to the public but well worth looking at from the gate on Main Street. The building dates from 1820 and with its palm-lined front garden has an air of mystique, as if it belongs instead to north Africa, or even to the deep south of the United States. Mystique is right; it was the setting for an inquiry into the disappearance of the *Marie Celeste*.

Main Street continues south, passing the Garrison Theatre and John Mackintosh Hall, another tribute to that colonial benefactor, then goes through the elegant Southport Gates, set into the lower end of the wall that King Charles V built in 1540.

Southport Gates King Carlos, to give him his Spanish name, ordered the original single gate and drawbridge in 1552, and he is remembered by his now eroding coat of arms set in the archway. Charles amended the

Royal arms by adding two columns representing the Pillars of Hercules and deleting *non* from the beginning of the Royal motto, making it *plus ultra*. After all, Spain was opening up vast territories in the Americas.

The second gate, beside it, was cut in 1883, and the large third gate in 1967.

Just inside the gates is a 30-ton muzzle-loading cannon standing as a stark reminder of the battles that have been fought in and around the Rock.

Trafalgar Cemetery And just outside the gates is the Trafalgar Cemetery, part of it occupying the only remaining section of King Charles's defensive ditch. The cemetery dates from around 1730 and its name is falsely emotive since only two victims of the Battle of Trafalgar lie here. East, above the cemetery, lies Prince Edward's Gate which takes us back into Town again; or west, are the Ragged Staff Gates which lead to Queensway and so back to where we started.

Ragged Staff Ragged Staff Gates may take their name from the emblem of wall-builder Charles V, though they could also be named from the flagstaff that marked the way for ships to come into the quay that stood immediately beyond the gates into British times. The modern Ragged Staff Wharf, like everything west of Line Wall Road, has been reclaimed from the Bay, some of it in the early days of this century. Indeed, Fish Market Arch which leads under Line Wall Road at the north end of Irish Town, led straight to the harbour when it was cut through the Moorish wall in 1903.

The dry dock, now run by Gibrepair

EUROPA AND THE HARBOUR

SOUTH from Southport all roads eventually lead to Europa Point. Beyond Harry's Bar and the Queen's Cinema is the bottom terminal of the Bland Line's cable car, built in the 1960s as a scenic way of taking tourists to the top of the spine of Gibraltar, more than 1,200 feet (400 metres) above the sea.

Alameda Gardens Beside the terminus are the Alameda Gardens, opened in 1816 and still one of the few places in Gibraltar where you can sit in the shade and enjoy a flower garden at any time of the year. Let us ignore the fact that the gardens are now misnamed, for *alameda* in Spanish means "poplar grove" (there are precious few poplars today), and look instead at the monument to General Eliott financed by his descendant Eliott Drake, who also claimed that Sir Francis Drake was among his ancestors.

The location is apt, since the gardens are on the site of the Red Sands, where Eliott assembled his troops for the night sortie during the Great Siege.

There's also a monument to the Duke of Wellington, but *that* was paid for by the compulsory deduction of a day's pay from every member of the Garrison. Wellington's bust was cast in bronze taken from some of the many cannon his troops captured.

Europa Road leads us on steeply, past the Casino, then gives us a choice: fork left up Engineer Road for the Upper Rock; straight on for Europa Point; or fork right down South Barrack Road for Rosia Bay, Camp Bay, and a backward look at the harbour.

Docks and Harbour Gibraltar would never have been an important military base without the means for the Navy to bring in the troops and ammunition. For quite a while after Rooke seized the Rock in 1704 the dockyard was a small affair, tucked in behind the stumpy New, or South Mole, where the dry docks are today.

Then in 1893 work began on the major project of creating a large, sheltered harbour west of the town. The South Mole crept northwards until it stretched 3,600 feet (1,100 metres) into the Bay; the North Mole grew westwards for 1,500 feet (450 m) as an island, connected to the stub of the old mole by the present viaduct (you'll not notice it unless you look carefully), then turned *south* and grew another 1,500 feet (500 m) under the name of the *Western* Arm, where the cruise liners moor today.

And between them grew the Detached Mole, 2,700 feet (820 m) of low wall closing the exposed western side of the harbour. In these 440 acres (178 hectares) of sheltered waters, merchant ships gathered into convoys for the Atlantic and the Mediterranean runs during the Second World War while their protection vessels moored at the North Mole jetties to be serviced. The three dry docks nearby were capable of taking the largest capital ships in the British Fleet; completed in 1905 they were declared redundant to naval needs 80 years later, and they're now run commercially by Gibrepair.

Hundred-ton Gun Overlooking Rosia Bay is the survivor of the two 100-ton guns mounted on the Rock in 1882 (the other was in the Alameda Gardens) two years after a British weapons manufacturer produced identical ordnances for the Italian Navy; the British installed two more monster cannon on Malta, for prudence.

This gun, one of the military attractions of the Rock, had a crew of 35 men, including a trumpeter, storeman, lampman, and a telephonist to take messages from the four range-finders. Its normal rate of fire was one 2,000 lb (around 900 kg) shell backed with 450 lb (200 kg) of powder, shot eight miles (13 km) at four-minute intervals, but one gunnery commander brought the rate of fire down to two and a half minutes – and split the barrel.

During a top-brass inspection in 1902 with a recast barrel, the gun failed to fire after a half-hour wait the general in command called for a volunteer to go head first down the 17.7 inch (450 mm) wide unrifled barrel and fix a rope to the eye-bolt in the cap of the shell. The trumpeter, the smallest member of the crew, volunteered...and was successful.

Camp Bay Beyond Rosia, and through a short tunnel, lies Camp Bay, with a beach, a jetty, and a shallow swimming pool for children. Further south lies Little Bay, also with a small beach and a pool. It also has a dramatic waterfall on the dry cliff face, but that's merely the outflow from the Glen Rocky Distillery. The name is clever, but there's no connection with whisky; the place distils fresh water from the sea.

The Hundred-ton Gun

Europa From Little Bay the road goes through the tunnel known as Keighley Way – there's a footpath along one side – and comes out on the Europa Flats, almost at the southern tip of the Rock.

Rubbish On the left, where Europa Advance Road appears to lead back to Catalan Bay (it doesn't: there's no entry for vehicles from this direction and no acces for pedestrians from either end), a forbidding steel doorway stands on the edge of the cliff. During the years when the frontier was closed the Gibraltarians disposed of their bulky and sinkable rubbish through these doors, behind which there's a 150 foot (50 m) drop straight into the sea.

Old cars, with oil and petrol drained, joined brick rubble and masonry in the final plunge, to be carried away by some of the strongest currents in the strait. Old cars still make their departure this way, but rubbish that would float or pollute is burned at the base of the North Cliff.

Evaporation in the Med is so great that there is, on average, a 2 knot (3 km-hr) current flowing eastwards through the strait at the surface, but there's a weaker counter-current 70 fathoms (150 m) down.

Lighthouse Trinity House, based in London, is responsible for maintaining all lighthouses, beacons and navigation aids in England, Wales, the Channel Islands...and this one at Europa Point in Gibraltar (the commissioners for Northern and for Irish lights share responsibility for the remainder of those in the British Isles).

The governor of the day, Sir Alexander Woodford, laid the foundation

Shrine of Our Lady – with whipping post

64

stone of the Europa Lighthouse on April 26, 1838, and the first light shone on August 1, 1841. It was from a single-wick oil lamp 150 feet (45 m) above the sea but improvements over the years have brought it, via a three-mantle oil lamp with a range of 18 miles (29 km) and later a single-mantle petrol-vapour lamp with a 39 inch (100 mm) lens, to the present 3 kw electric light with a revolving lens giving an occulting beam visible for 30 miles (48 km). The modern light is also a little higher at 61 feet (18 m) above base rock, and 156 feet (47 m) above high water. And in this part of the world, high water is only around three feet (one metre) above low water.

Europa's light also has twin foghorns, for there are days when a thick mist fills the strait, with only the tip of Mount Abyla – Ape's Hill in Morocco – rising clear from it. Yet there are other days when you can pick out detail on the beaches in Africa, 12 and more miles distant.

Our Lady of Europa The lighthouse was not the first beacon to burn on Europa Point to help passing sailors. The Moors built a mosque 500 yards (metres) north-west of where the lighthouse now stands, and sometime after 1462, when the Duke of Medina Sidonia recaptured El Peñon, the Spanish converted the mosque into the Shrine of Nuestra Señora de Europa and burned lamps there, day and night, signalling not only the presence of the shrine to worshippers from the town, but also the presence of the Rock to sailors already dangerously close inshore.

Nuestra Señora, "Our Lady," was venerated in a small wooden image of the Virgin Mary which took place of honour in the shrine.

Our Lady has had a troubled life. When Barbarossa's Turks landed at Europa in 1540 and went on a day's rampage, they sacked the church. But in 1704, when Sir George Rooke seized the Rock for the Spanish Pretender, Carlos III, his soldiers plundered the shrine and threw the Virgin Mary into the sea, a strange action for troops who were not supposed to be putting down Catholicism in favour of Protestantism.

Father Romero, a priest who bravely saw his duty of protecting the Catholic Cathedral as more important than escaping to San Roque, recovered the damaged statue and smuggled it to Algeciras.

When the British went on a purge of Gibraltar's religious buildings, using them for more prosaic purposes, they turned the Shrine of Our Lady of Europa into a barrack and guardhouse, and put up a whipping-post just outside the door: it's there today as a grim reminder of the barbarity of military life not so long ago.

In May 1864 Bishop Scandella brought Our Lady back to Gibraltar, with the Army providing a guard of honour from Waterport to the Governor's residence, the former Convent. The statue then went to the specially-built Chapel of Our Little Sisters of the Poor where it stayed for 75 years until the start of the Second World War.

Under Hitler's menace the Virgin Mary, by now regarded as the patroness of Gibraltar, took quarters in the Catholic Cathedral, then in August 1954 moved on in torchlit procession to St Joseph's Church in Rodgers Road, as the Army was still using the shrine down at Europa. By

Queen's Road on the Upper Rock

1961 the Army had moved out and on October 17 of that year the shrine was again available as a church. On September 28, 1962, the first Mass was celebrated there since 1704, and on October 7, 1968, Our Lady of Europa at last came home, once more in stately procession.

UPPER ROCK

IF WE had taken the left fork at the Casino, Engineer's Road would have put us on route to pass within a few feet of the topmost point of Gibraltar, 1,396 ft (425.5 m) above sea level. And the climb would have been spectacular whichever route we took.

There's no subtlety about it: Engineer's Road is ankle-achingly steep and as we cross the 500 foot (150 m) contour we can look down on an eerie landscape where several acres of the limestone have been stripped of vegetation, plastered over, and painted white. They are the first of the rain catchments which channel water into gutters and carry it, via tunnels, deep into the Rock for storage. But these are small and for the military; the main catchments are still ahead.

Engineer's Road meets Queen's Road at an abrupt hairpin bend almost 600 feet (200 m) above the sea, offering an observation platform with views to the south, towards the strait and Africa. You must ignore the road that plunges over the edge towards the Windmill flats; it's one of several military routes that are still closed to the civilian population.

Mediterranean Steps If you're a keen hill walker you'll thrill at the challenge of the Mediterranean Steps which lead up from here, round the eastern face of the Rock, to meet tarmac again at the top of O'Hara's Road, not far from the highest point.

It's not a dangerous route but you need to be prepared for it; high heels and tight skirts are out of the question and there are several sections where it's useful to have both hands free. Some of the steps are hewn from stone, some are cast in concrete with a handrail fitted, but there are also stretches of bare path – and all the way you have magnificent views reaching from the snowy peaks of the Sierra Nevada to the mountains of The Rif in Morocco.

Queen's Road Or there's the more sedate approach along Queen's Road, still steep, but walkable. Traffic flows in one direction on this road and as that's from behind, it's advisable to be ready to step aside. On the steeper grades as taxis grind past, you may notice large iron rings set into the rock face beside the road. Spare a thought for the men of byegone generations who fixed pulleys to these rings and hauled cannon and ammunition up these slopes purely by muscle power and body weight.

Soon you have another choice. Cave Branch Road leads off to the right, meets O'Hara's Road and continues to the top of the Mediterranean Steps, via St Michael's Cave and The Cabin restaurant.

St Michael's Cave The cave is one of the natural showpieces of the Rock, with stalactites hundreds of thousands of years old hanging from the roof. One which broke free long before the first man set foot on Tarik's Mountain has been cemented to the floor by natural accretion and its polished stump, trimmed in 1972, shows a cross-section of geological history which some people believe even records the Ice Ages.

The unplumbed depths of St Michael's Cave probably gave rise to the story of a tunnel connecting Gibraltar with Ape's Hill in Morocco, through which the Barbary apes made their perilous journey to Europe.

Apes' Den Back along Queen's Road, the next call is the Apes' Den where you're confronted with fact and legend yet again. These tailless monkeys - they're not apes at all – are the only wild primates in Europe excluding *homo sapiens* himself. They obviously didn't come to the Rock through the fanciful tunnel, though their origins are unknown. But as legend claims that the British will leave Gibraltar if ever the "apes" die out, Winston Churchill, calling here on his way to the Teheran Conference during the Second World War, decreed that their numbers, then dangerously down to seven, be increased to 35 by bringing in fresh stock from Morocco.

As the nineteenth-century human population of the Rock increased, so the macaque monkeys were driven onto the barren upper slopes. Reluctant to live on a spartan diet they often raided the town and a colonel of the Royal Engineers lodged a claim when the monkeys ravaged his garden, frightened his children, tore up his trousers and even slept in his bed.

Later, the "apes" became War Office responsibility and the Gibraltar

Estimates allowed for the cost of their rations, standing at fourpence (just under two decimal pence) per animal per day in 1951. The commanding officer of the Gibraltar Regiment, a battallion of part-time soldiers, now carries the odd title of Officer in Charge of the Apes, and he is responsible for ensuring they're fed – at 8am and 4pm – and billetted in their cages at the den.

Visitors intent on feeding members of this pack of monkeys should confine their offerings to fruit and nuts, and hold onto their cameras and handbags while doing so. There's a second pack running much wilder on Middle Hill and you'll not get close enough to any of them to feed them.

The male macaque matures at five years, usually surviving no longer than 17 years, but Jacko lived to 21, dying in the London Zoo. The females mature at four and may produce one infant a year for five years.

The Army, anxious to avoid having monkeys go absent without leave, gives each one a name and records its birth and any significant incidents during its life, but can only presume death when the animal ceases to come for its daily ration for no trace of any dead monkey has ever been found on the Rock, leading to the belief that the animals have their own secret burial ground.

Charles V's Wall From the Apes' Den there's yet another chance to scale the topmost ridge of the Rock, accessible this time by the steps built into the top of Charles V's Wall. If you make it, there's a short walk along St Michael's Road (no vehicles allowed) to the upper station of the Bland Cable Car and the snack bar which is on top at rock bottom.

Rain Catchments From up here, astride the razorback ridge of Gibraltar, there's a dramatic view down to Catalan Bay and the rain catchments which dominate the eastern slope of the Rock.

Finding sufficient fresh water has always been a problem on Gibraltar, with early wells on the isthmus soon turning brackish due to over-pumping. In 1903 the first wooden stakes were driven into the scree above Catalan Bay, the first sheets of corrugated iron fixed to them, and the first of the autumn rains were captured in gutters at the bottom, rather as one would take water from a roof. The idea worked, and within a few years the catchments covered 30 acres (12 hectares) of scree, providing a landmark visible from miles away.

More to the point, the catchments provide a fair proportion of the Rock's drinking water, though supplies vary with the seasons. One inch (25 mm) of rain falling vertically on the catchments gives 650,000 gallons (3,000 hectolitres) of water, so an average annual rainfall of 30 inches (760 mm) would yield 19,500,000 gallons, more than enough for the 16,000,000 gallon 730,000,000 hl) capacity of the 13 reservoirs carved in the Rock between 1898 and 1961.

But as there's no regular rainfall in the summer and the demand far exceeds this figure, there's still the need for distillation from sea water, for fresh water from the 19 shallow wells on the isthmus which yield around 750,000 gallons a week, and even then there's occasional call for a tanker-load of drinking water shipped in from, of all places, Morocco.

And it's still not enough. Throughout Gibraltar, all lavatories flush with water drawn from the sea.

Back on the Upper Rock, Queen's Road ends abruptly at an observation platform on the lip of the North Face, giving breezy views of the isthmus around 500 feet (150 m) below, and extending beyond the frontier to take in La Línea de la Concepción, the little town of San Roque, and the rolling mountains of Cádiz province.

Upper Galleries A mercifully short stretch of road takes us to the Upper Galleries, the handiwork of Sergeant Major Ince during the Great Siege. The tunnel and its gun emplacements have changed little since those days, and recently the London costumiers Berman and Nathan have supplied lifelike models of several people who played an important part in the three-year struggle. General Eliott is here, conferring with Ince, while in another gallery are the lads Richardson and Brand, better known as Shot and Shell, who were attached to the Soldier Artificer Company during the siege. Their sight was so keen they could spot the blast from Spanish cannon and report the direction of the incoming shells.

From St George's Hall, where cannon still stand at the ready, the concrete-floored Holyland Tunnel leads out to the eastern face and offers yet another dramatic view of the rain catchments above Catalan Bay.

Ince's Farm Down from the galleries, if we'd gone back along Queen's Road to just past its junction with Old Queen's Road, we would have seen a plot of precipitous rock partly overgrown with wild bamboo. Somewhere in the vegetation is a sign which proclaims this as Ince's Farm, a dubious

View of La Línea de la Concepción

gift for the man whose genius created those splendid galleries.

Down again properly on Willis's Road, we pass the entrance to four of the Rock's 13 reservoirs as we approach the Moorish Castle.

Tower of Homage The Tower of Homage is the only part of the castle still carrying a roof, and it was in this small section that Estevan de Villacreces survived for five months during the ninth siege while the Duke of Medina Sidonia tried to recapture his possessions.

Estevan is still here today, perpetuated in wax and sharing space with Tarik ibn Zeyad, the man who gave his name to the Rock. It's a fitting location for the disciple of Islam who did more than any other man to threaten the existence of Christianity.

AT SEA LEVEL

GIBRALTAR'S best sands are on the Eastern Beach, which stretches from the site of the Devil's Tower to the southern edge of the runway. Catalan Bay and Sandy Bay, also on the Mediterranean side, are smaller and are backed up with ice-cream stalls instead of the parked lorries behind Eastern Beach. Catalan and Sandy bays also trap the morning sun, but by mid afternoon the shadow of the Rock begins to creep over them.

On the Atlantic side Camp Bay has the only beach, with a shallow pool for children and the usual holiday amenities. Little Bay to the south mainly offers swimming from the rocks, and beachless Rosia Bay is reserved for military personnel.

Beware the warning of the red flag. Whenever this is flying on any beach swimming is forbidden and if you escape the currents you're likely to catch a fine. The Police Office in Irish Town also lists any beaches temporarily unsafe.

Currents? Just think about it: Gibraltar is where the tidal Atlantic meets the almost tideless Mediterranean. Millons of tons of water surge eastward through the strait on every incoming tide.

Much of this water flows back again with the receding tide, the loss explained by evaporation in the Mediterranean. A slight change in wind or ocean current is enough to bring this mass of water too close for safety.

Fishing The fish don't mind the currents; their problem is the anglers. Tuna have been plentiful in the Atlantic for centuries and the Romans stamped their effigy on the coins they minted at nearby Carteia. There are also plenty of bream and red mullet, bonito and mackerel, with little scarcity of rock cod, sole, turbot, swordfish, flying fish, and conger eels. Even the peculiar John Dory has been landed, though one of the biggest single catches to come ashore at Gibraltar was a stone bass in 1963, weighing 80 lb 4 oz (36.39 kg).

The motor launch *Coronia*, which Dunkirk veterans may remember as the little ship *Watchful*, cruises daily around the Rock with the near certainty of seeing dolphins at play. Occasionally its passengers may see something not quite so welcome: the blue shark.

living Rock

GIBRALTAR is on one of the main bird migration routes of the world and millions cross from Africa to Europe between February and May to return south between late July and October. They come in two distinct streams; the soaring birds, including most of the raptors and the white storks, by day, gaining height over one continent and crossing the strait on a long and gentle glide. The watcher sitting on the Upper Rock in spring with a good pair of binoculars will therefore see large birds coming in quite low, either in small groups or, in the case of the honey buzzard, in flocks of up to 1,500.

The smaller birds, who must cross the water by muscle power, usually come at night and fly higher; often the only hint of their passing is their song drifting down from the darkness.

The main migrants which the visitor can hope to see are the honey buzzard, the black kite, the short-toed and the booted eagle, the sparrow hawk and Montagu's harrier, with occasional glimpses of the red kite, osprey, marsh and hen harrier, and the goshawk. Non-raptors include the skylark, the swallow – though many of these come up Italy or risk overflying the gun-happy Lebanese – corn bunting, wheatear, redstart, chiff-chaff and willow warbler, all of which make it to northern Europe. The more exotic migrants, the bee-eater, the hoopoe and the golden oriole, stay in southern Europe.

White storks nest in plenty in the towns around Cádiz, going inland as far as Badajoz, but they prefer to cross the strait near Tarifa.

Gibraltar has few resident birds but can claim one that is found nowhere else in Europe: the Barbary partridge, *caccabis petrosa*, has not even bothered to fly along the isthmus to La Línea. Bonelli's eagle, the Egyptian vulture and the peregrine falcon have occasionally nested on the Upper Rock but prefer the wilder country of Spain.

The Rock also has a unique plant, *iberis gibraltarica*, the Gibraltar candytuft, which is plentiful at both ends of the Upper Rock in spring, particularly near the top of the Mediterranean Steps. Poor soil on the higher parts of Gibraltar limits the scope for wild plants but there is a scrub vegetation of wild olive, with outbursts of locust bean known in Spain as *algorrobo* and known to British children a generation ago as a substitute for chocolates. There's also fig, orange, lemon, almond, eucalyptus, Scots pine and Californian cypress and, in the town, the date palm. The fruit seldom ripens in Gibraltar but in Elche, Spain, date palms grow as weeds.

Gibraltar also has the unusual *mimosa pudica*, the sensitive plant, a few examples of the African acacia with thorns up to two inches (6 cm) long; there are several good examples of prickly pear cactus – the leaves when lightly cooked taste like broad beans, and the Spaniards make jam of the fruits – and a hardy mesembryanthemum has colonised the windswept Europa Point.

Around 1,400 species of beetle have been found in the Campo, including the dung beetle and the cockroach, this latter known in Spain as the *cucuracha* where it was formerly kept in small cages for its song. The Campo has also yielded 57 species of butterfly with 34 of them, including the swallowtail, found on the Rock.

Scorpions are very rare in Gibraltar and Spain, but abound in Morocco. Locusts are infrequent visitors but you may occasionally see centipedes up to six inches (15 cm) long. There's no shortage of lizards on the Rock – in earlier times the inhabitants called themselves Rock scorpions or lizards – but you'll have to go to Spain to see a big one. You won't find any big snakes on the Rock either, and the small ones are non-poisonous. If you see something which looks like a snake but moves far too slowly, look again: it's probably a procession of caterpillars going head-to-tail and trying to fool those hungry migrating birds.

Small-boat marina

Holiday Rock

HERE'S a suggested itinerary for a week's holiday in Gibraltar, assuming you are staying in the town.

MONDAY morning: get the feel of the place. Walk from the sundial roundabout on Winston Churchill Avenue to the Southport Gates. *Afternoon*: take a bus or taxi to the Upper Rock and back, then bus or taxi clockwise round the Rock via Devil's Tower Road, Catalan Bay, Europa Point and back to town. *Evening*: see Gibraltar television in your hotel, go to the cinema, try a pub or fish and chips.

TUESDAY morning: do a little shopping, but make certain you're in Convent Place well before 10.20 for the Changing of the Guard. Consider a day in either Spain or Morocco for Thursday and make arrangements. *Afternoon*: take cable car to the top of the Rock, walk along and explore the Upper Galleries and the Moorish Castle. *Evening*: try the Casino.

WEDNESDAY morning: take a town tour, including Casemates Square, Waterport, museum and cathedrals, the Trafalgar Cemetery and ending in the Alameda Gardens. Bus back. *Afternoon*: take bus or taxi to Europa Point and walk back, via the Shrine of Our Lady, Rosia Bay and the 100-ton Gun. A lot of walking, but little climbing. *Evening*: Harry's Trafalgar Bar.

THURSDAY: day trip. Morocco by Gibair (going by sea calls for a night in Africa which is too long for a week's holiday). Or Spain, by coach from Gibraltar, with destinations as far as Cádiz, Jerez or Málaga. Or hire a car either in Gibraltar or La Línea and go as you please. Or walk, with San Roque your maximum range.

FRIDAY: taxi to St Michael's Cave, walk on to top of O'Hara's Road and think about coming down via the Mediterrnean Steps – or Charles V's Wall. Take in the Apes' Den and come back to town via the footpath to Flat Bastion Road. *Late afternoon and evening*: rest.

SATURDAY morning: cruise in MV Caronia or take hydrofoil to Algeciras and back. *Afternoon*: complete your shopping.

SUNDAY morning: bus to Catalan Bay; walk on to Sandy Bay and then back to town. *Afternoon*: walk out to western arm of North Mole for view of Rock and the shipping *Evening*: church.

The only fixed item in this itinerary is the Changing of the Guard on Tuesday, but it's not a good idea to visit Morocco on Friday, the Islamic holy day. Apart from that, there are innumerable variations on the theme, with the prospect of diving with Gibaqua, joining the Windsurfing School, going sea angling or sailing, attending a philatelic conference or spending every day stretched out on the beach. One thing is certain, however: it'll be a unique experience. Nowhere else in the world can offer the combination that's available on the Rock – the English language and British coinage, bobbies and postmen, mixed with the summer sunshine that only the Mediterranean can guarantee. At Rock Bottom in Europe, you'll feel on top of the world!

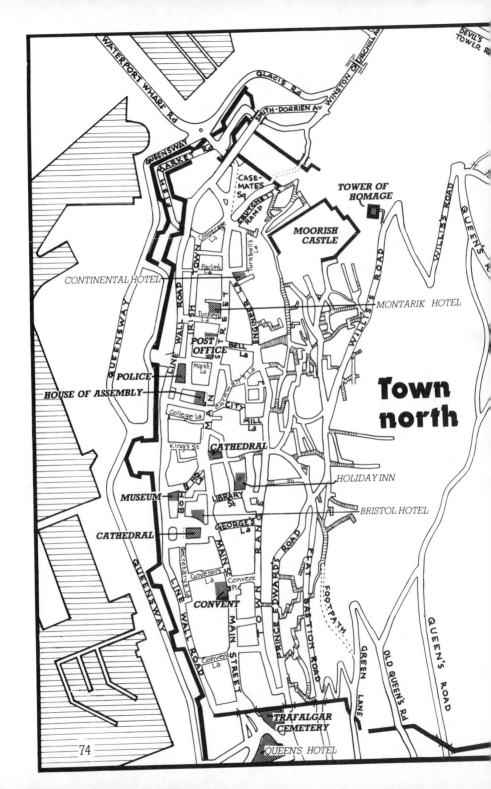

Town north

TRAFALGAR CEMETERY

74

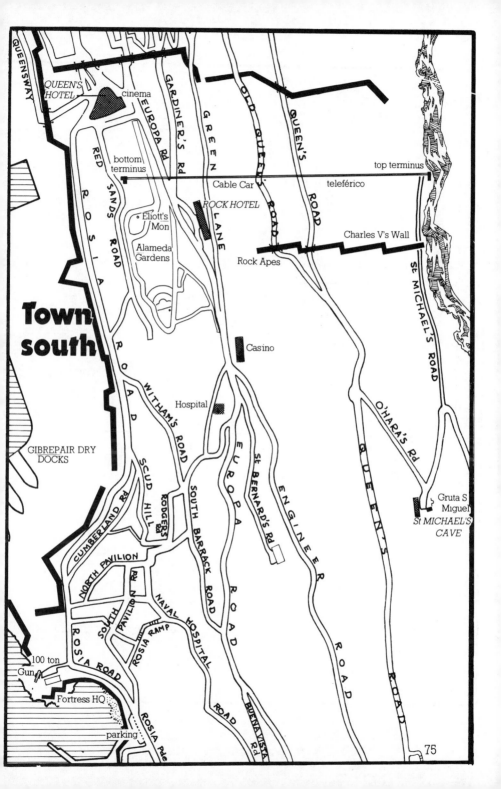

QUEENSWAY

QUEEN'S HOTEL

cinema

EUROPA Rd.

GARDINER'S Rd.

GREEN LANE

OLD QUEEN'S ROAD

QUEEN'S ROAD

RED SANDS ROAD

ROSIA ROAD

bottom terminus

top terminus

Cable Car   teleférico

ROCK HOTEL

Eliott's Mon

Alameda Gardens

Charles V's Wall

Rock Apes

St MICHAEL'S ROAD

Town south

Casino

WITHAM'S ROAD

Hospital

EUROPA ROAD

St BERNARD'S Rd.

ENGINEER ROAD

O'HARA'S Rd.

QUEEN'S ROAD

GIBREPAIR DRY DOCKS

SCUD HILL

CUMBERLAND Rd.

RODGERS Rd.

NORTH PAVILION

SOUTH PAVILION

NAVAL HOSPITAL ROAD

SOUTH BARRACK ROAD

ROSIA RAMP

BUENA VISTA Rd.

Gruta S Miguel

St MICHAEL'S CAVE

100 ton Gun

Fortress HQ

ROSIA ROAD

ROSIA Rde.

parking

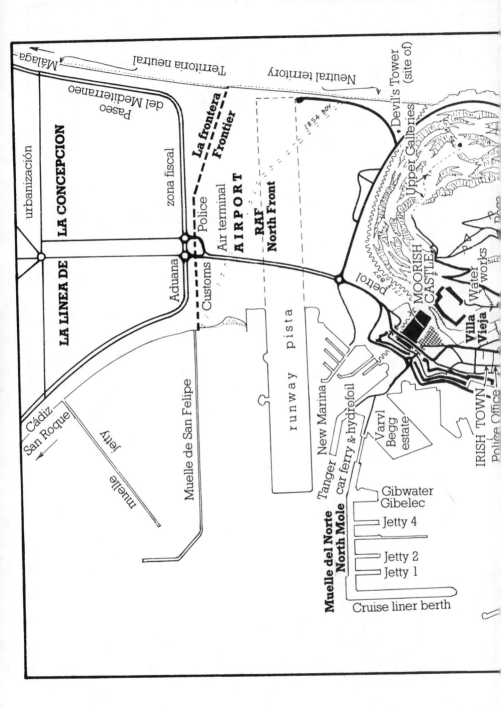

Malaga

Territoria neutral

Neutral territory

Devil's Tower (site of)

Paseo del Mediterraneo

Upper Galleries

La frontera
Frontier

urbanización

zona fiscal

1854 bry

Police

Air terminal

AIRPORT

RAF
North Front

LA LINEA DE LA CONCEPCION

Aduana

Customs

MOORISH CASTLE

Villa Vieja

Water works

Petrol

runway   pista

Cádiz
San Roque

Muelle de San Felipe

IRISH TOWN

Police Office

muelle jetty

jetty

New Marina

Tanger
car ferry & hydrofoil

Varyl Begg estate

Gibwater
Gibelec

Jetty 4

Muelle del Norte
North Mole

Jetty 2

Jetty 1

Cruise liner berth

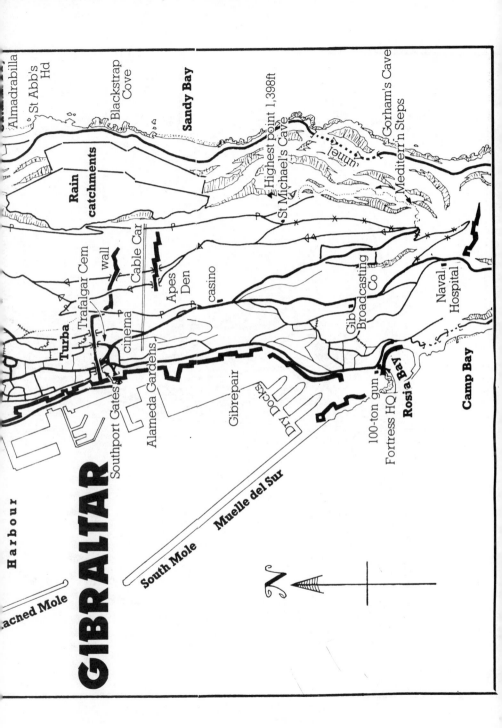

GIBRALTAR

Harbour

...ached Mole

South Mole

Muelle del Sur

Turba

Southport Gates
cinema
Trafalgar Cem
wall
Alameda Gardens
Cable Car
Apes Den
casino
Gibrepair
Dry Docks
100-ton gun
Fortress HQ
Rosia Bay
Gib Broadcasting Co
Naval Hospital
Camp Bay

Rain catchments

Almadrabilla
St Abb's Hd
Blackstrap Cove
Sandy Bay
Highest point 1,398ft
St Michael's Cave
tunnel
Gorham's Cave
Mediterr'n Steps

N

77

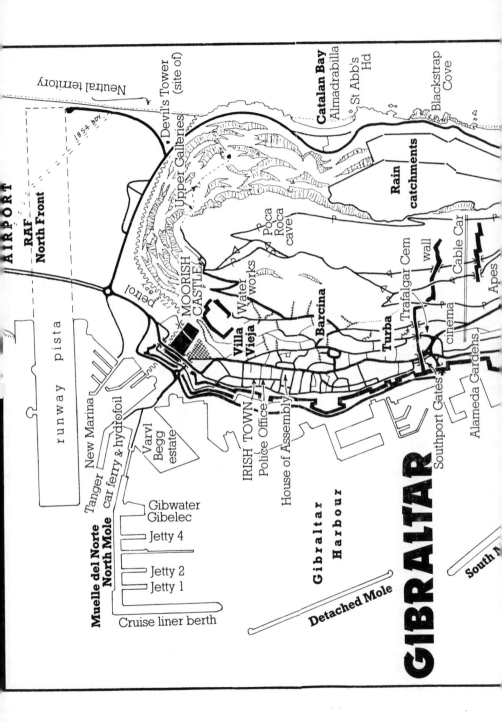

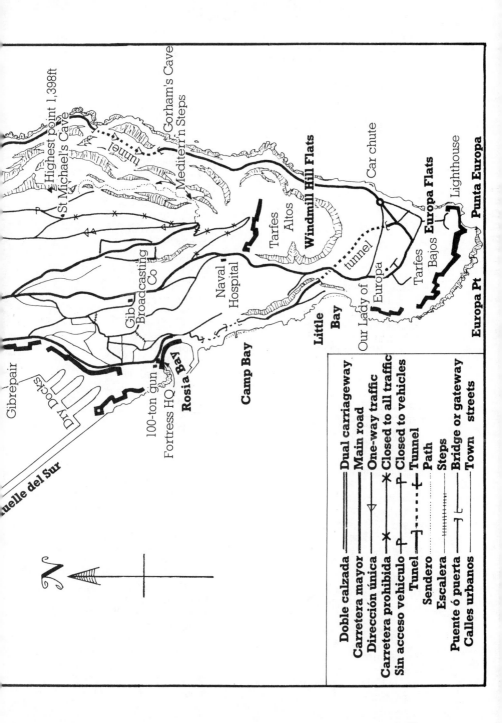

Doble calzada ═══ Dual carriageway
Carretera mayor ━━━ Main road
Dirección única ▽ One-way traffic
Carretera prohibida ✕ Closed to all traffic
Sin acceso vehículo ⌐ Closed to vehicles
Tunel ╪ Tunnel
Sendero ⋯⋯ Path
Escalera ╫╫╫ Steps
Puente ó puerta ┐┌ Bridge or gateway
Calles urbanos ━━ Town streets

Highest point 1,398ft
St Michael's Cave
Gorham's Cave
Mediterr'n Steps
tunnel
Windmill Hill Flats
Car chute
Tarfes Altos
Gib Broadcasting Co
Naval Hospital
Tarfes Bajos
Europa Flats
Lighthouse
Punta Europa
tunnel
Our Lady of Europa
Little Bay
Europa Pt
Camp Bay
Rosia Bay
100-ton gun
Fortress HQ
Gibrepair
Dry Docks
uelle del Sur

N

INDEX